THE CALCULATING COOK

a gourmet cookbook
for diabetics & dieters

by Jeanne Jones

**drawings
by Holly Zapp**

**101 Productions
San Francisco**

APPROVED FOR USE BY DIABETICS BY

THE AMERICAN DIABETES ASSOCIATION, NEW YORK

Also by Jeanne Jones

SECRETS OF SALT FREE COOKING
A complete low-sodium cookbook

DIET FOR A HAPPY HEART
A low-cholesterol, low-saturated-fat, low-calorie cookbook

FABULOUS FIBER COOKBOOK
Foods high in dietary fiber, low in calories and completely natural

Tenth Printing: December, 1978

Distributed to the book trade in the United States
by Charles Scribner's Sons, New York

Library of Congress Catalog Card Number 72-77564
ISBN 912238-23-2

PUBLISHED BY 101 PRODUCTIONS
834 Mission Street
San Francisco, California 94103

contents

TO KAKI
for constant encouragement

In Grateful Acknowledgement:
Johanna Nelson, R.D. for technical advice and professional assistance.
Susan Way for manuscript preparation on the revised edition.
Joy Kirkpatrick, R.D. for professional assistance with the revised edition.
Mildred Mead for being the most imaginative cook I know.
Robert Letts Jones for invaluable editorial help.

11th Edition, "Food Values of Portions Commonly Used"
by Bowes & Church, J.B. Lippincott Company

Recently an attractive passenger gazed with awe into the cockpit of a 747 airliner. "How in the world can you understand that maze of instruments?" she asked. Without a moment's hesitation the captain leaned back toward the passenger and, shading his mouth as though he were telling a secret, he whispered, "Decals, ma'am, just decals. Under the dash is a button labeled 'Honolulu' and we just press it!"

As physicians, we have spent years in research on the subjects of diabetes, weight reduction and just plain healthful living. The results are an accumulation of voluminous statistics that leave the average person lost in a veritable maze of information. Jeanne Jones, THE CALCULATING COOK, has pressed the button labeled "Gourmet Dining" and out of the maze we are on our way to a new experience in gastronomic enjoyment. Rather than pouring over the necessary statistics we can now enjoy dining and, coincidentally, be scientifically accurate in doing so.

Reading the galley proofs for this book started my mouth watering. I so vividly recalled the many gourmet dinners I have enjoyed in Jeanne Jones' home. Every meal I shared was a work of art. I can still hardly believe the number of years I enjoyed these epicurean delights before I knew or even suspected that she was a diabetic. Her cooking is a delight for anyone to enjoy, diabetic or not. With her help you no longer need to hide poor cooking behind the excuse of a restricted diet.

THE CALCULATING COOK is now sharing her secrets. Fly along with her into a culinary world of boundless horizons.

Carmel, California

BON APPETIT!
Eric G. Tarr, M.D.

introduction

I love to cook and to entertain. I especially enjoy giving small dinner parties created around eight guests.

I like to vary the mood from one dinner party to the next and let the food match the occasion. Sometimes for very casual dinners, I serve only one course, consisting of corned beef and cabbage, home-made rye bread and baked apples for dessert. Other times, for more formal dinner parties, I serve many courses with at least two different kinds of wine and end dramatically with a flaming dessert.

Because I have always loved to cook and to delight my friends with the results, I have gone to several French cooking schools. I learned how to make all of my own stocks and sauces, how to blend herbs and spices for the best results, and how to present foods so that they are beautiful as well as delicious. But, most important of all, I acquired the background necessary for using my own imagination in the kitchen, and that is when the fun in cooking really begins.

About the time I had been cooking and entertaining long enough and successfully enough so that I was beginning to think of myself as somewhat of a professional, I ran into a shocking problem. I discovered I had diabetes!

I had not been feeling well, and went to see my doctor for an examination. When he had gotten all of my test results back, I returned to his office. "Jeanne," he said, "You have diabetes!" He might just as well have told me that I had leprosy for the effect it had on me.

I turned pale, collapsed in the chair and looked at my doctor in disbelief, but he went right on talking. "I am going to give you a diet program to follow. It is called an Exchange Diet. It was designed to help diabetics easily understand exactly how much of various foods they are allowed to eat at each meal. However, it is the best diet in the world for anyone who wants to control his weight for any reason, and if you want to start feeling better and control your diabetes, you had better stick to it."

I was scared. First of all because diabetes sounded like such a terrible problem, but even worse, I felt my life was ruined. How could I give lovely, gourmet dinner parties when I had been put on a diet that I had never even heard of before, without sugar, with practically no fats and measured amounts of almost everything else!

One day while I was sitting, crying in my kitchen, an encouraging thought came to me. If I could adjust my favorite recipes, and work out new ones, so that I knew exactly how much of everything was in each portion, I could still cook very exciting food and stay completely on the diet program at the same time, and so could anyone else using my recipes. That was the day I stopped crying and became THE CALCULATING COOK.

I cooked and tasted and weighed and measured for months. Many things I threw away; others, the recipes you will find in this book, I wrote down to remember.

Many friends who had always loved coming to my house for dinner seemed to enjoy coming even more. A few of them told me that previously they had always felt they had to give up eating, either two days before or two days after one of my meals. Now they eat the food I serve with even greater relish, knowing that they are not putting on extra pounds at the same time.

I have become fascinated with a whole new concept in cooking. The constant challenge of trying to balance recipes, so that they work out in easily calculated exchanges without losing anything in flavor, is actually making cooking more fun for me than it ever was before. Plus, I eat just as well and entertain just as successfully.

Why not let me help you be a CALCULATING COOK, to feel better, look younger and live longer!

—JEANNE JONES

the exchange diet program

The Exchange Diet Program is a system of grouping foods according to the amounts of carbohydrates, protein, fat and calories they contain. There are six basic types of foods:

1—Foods containing only carbohydrates are called FRUIT EX-CHANGES or FRUIT PORTIONS.

2—Foods containing carbohydrates and small amounts of protein are called BREAD EXCHANGES or STARCH PORTIONS.

3—Foods containing larger amounts of carbohydrates and protein are called VEGETABLE EXCHANGES or VEGETABLE PORTIONS.

4—Foods containing nearly equal amounts of carbohydrates and proteins are called MILK EXCHANGES or MILK PORTIONS. They are divided into three groups: non-fat, low-fat and whole, depending on the amount of fat each contains.

5—Foods containing protein and some fat are called MEAT EX-CHANGES or PROTEIN PORTIONS. They are also divided into three groups: low-fat, medium-fat and high-fat, depending on the amount of fat each contains.

6—Foods containing mostly fat are called FAT EXCHANGES or FAT PORTIONS.

Exchange is the term given to a specified amount of a certain type of food. One Exchange may be "exchanged" for any other specified amount within the same group because it has the same food value and the same number of calories. For example: 1 small apple is listed as 1 Fruit Exchange; 1/2 small banana is also 1 Fruit Exchange. If you are allowed only 1 Fruit Exchange for lunch you may want 1 small apple or you may want only 1/2 apple and 1/4 small banana, which also equals 1 Fruit Exchange. It doesn't matter which fruit or fruits you choose so long as the amount you eat adds up to 1 Fruit Exchange.

The same thing is true of all the Exchange lists. The Bread

Exchange list gives 1 slice of bread as 1 Bread Exchange. 1 Bread Exchange can also be 1/2 cup cooked oatmeal. If you are allowed only 1 Bread Exchange for breakfast, you may want 1 slice of bread toasted or you may want 1/2 cup oatmeal instead. If you want both the toast and oatmeal, you can only have 1/2 slice toast and 1/4 cup oatmeal which added together equal 1 Bread Exchange.

As a general rule, trades should not be made between the different Exchange groups. However, it is good to know which food groups can be exchanged for other food groups in cases of emergencies.

The easiest interchange between the Exchange lists is for Fruit and Bread Exchanges. Also it is the most frequently necessary for emergencies.

1 Fruit Exchange = 2/3 Bread Exchange

1 Bread Exchange = 1-1/2 Fruit Exchanges

For example: If fruit were not available you could eat 2/3 slice of bread instead of the fruit. Or if you needed another Bread Exchange, you could eat 3 tablespoons raisins instead of 1/2 English muffin or 1-1/2 Fruit Exchanges instead of 1 Bread Exchange!

You can also interchange Bread Exchanges with Vegetable Exchanges.

1 Vegetable Exchange = 1/3 Bread Exchange

1 Bread Exchange = 3 Vegetable Exchanges

For example: you can substitute 1/3 cup cooked rice for 1/2 cup beets or have 1-1/2 cups cooked carrots instead of 1 slice bread.

One 8-ounce glass of low-fat milk equals 1 Low-fat Milk Exchange and may be substituted for 1 Bread Exchange plus 1 Low-fat Meat Exchange. Or, if you don't have the milk, you may have 1 generous Fruit Exchange plus 1 Low-fat Meat Exchange. See why you often hear milk called the complete food!

Remember these interchanges are for emergencies only and should not be used all of the time.

Sound complicated? Well, it certainly did to me, but you will be amazed how quickly and easily it will become very simple and almost second nature to remember exact portions.

I also have worked with dietitians to greatly expand the Exchange lists for you. You will find them in the following chapter.

When I was given my Exchange list it said, "Eat only those foods which are on your list." Now, I knew that couldn't be true! After all, practically everything has a measurable amount of food value and therefore can be given an Exchange value. So we have worked out the Exchanges for everything we could think of that you might want to eat and listed it in a greatly expanded, more helpful and much less frustrating Exchange list than the printed ones your doctor has given you.

This diet allows you to measure foods rather than weighing them. Therefore, it is just as easy to eat the proper amounts when you are away from home. You will be amazed at how quickly you can sight-guess the amounts of food allowed very accurately. This allows you to eat in restaurants with very few problems.

When eating in restaurants it is always best to order "straight-forward" food, such as steak, lamb chops, broiled lobster, fish or chicken. Ask for your meat broiled without added butter and your potato "au naturel." If you order foods prepared in sauce, it is difficult to calculate the exact Exchanges.

When you are a guest in someone's home, you can usually eat most of what you are served. And at dessert time, for heaven's sake don't go into your medical history! Just tell your hostess that her dinner was so delicious you have already eaten too much and couldn't possibly eat one more thing!

exchange diet

Your doctor will give you the Exchange Diet calorie level that he wants you to follow. You may already have one of those cute little charts which is almost impossible to read. To simplify your diet program for you, I have listed the most frequently prescribed Exchange Diets from 800 calories per day through 3000 calories per day. With each caloric level I have given you a sample menu for 3 days to give you a better idea of how to use the Exchange Lists. These diets follow the Exchange lists.

The foods listed for each day must be evenly divided among the allowed meals for that day. The only exceptions are the Fat Exchanges. They may be saved up during the day, but only for one day, and eaten all at one meal. Just think! This means that sometimes you can have real whipped cream on your strawberries and more than 1 teaspoon mayonnaise with cold, cracked crab.

The Exchange Diet is not any mysterious cure for diabetes. The main purpose of the Exchange Diet is to help you control your weight while eating a perfectly balanced diet for your nutritional needs. Weight control is an extremely important factor in the control of diabetes.

Although this diet was designed for diabetics, it is now used by some of the world's leading health spas for weight-control programs.

Most doctors recommend a vitamin supplement for all diets under 1200 calories per day. It is always advisable to consult a doctor before going on any diet for any reason.

This book will also be very helpful to anyone who wants to control his weight in a sensible, interesting and delicious fashion.

Remember, changing your eating habits temporarily will change your weight. But if you want to keep that gorgeous new body, you must make those new eating habits a permanent part of your life.

FRUIT EXCHANGE LIST

Each portion below equals
1 Fruit Exchange and contains
approximately:
10 grams of carbohydrate
40 calories

Apple: 1 2 inches in diameter
Apple juice: 1/2 cup
Applesauce, unsweetened:
    1/2 cup
Apricots, fresh: 2 medium**
Apricots, dried: 3 halves**
Avocado: see Fat Exchange List
Banana: 1/2 small
Blackberries: 1/2 cup
Blueberries: 1/2 cup
Cantaloupe: 1/4 6 inches in
    diameter***
Cherries, sweet: 10 large
Cranberries, unsweetened: unlimited
Crenshaw melon: 2-inch wedge
Dates: 2
Date "sugar": 1 tablespoon
Figs, fresh: 1 large
Figs, dried: 1 large
Fructose: 1 tablespoon
Grapefruit: 1/2 4 inches in diameter*
Grapefruit juice: 1/2 cup*
Grapes: 12 large
Grapes, Thompson Seedless:
    20 grapes
Grape juice: 1/4 cup
Guava: 2/3*
Honeydew melon: 1/4 5 inches
    in diameter

Kumquats: 2
Lemon juice: 1/2 cup
Lime juice: 1/2 cup
Loquats: 3
Lychees, fresh: 3
Mango: 1/2 small**
Nectarine: 1 medium
Orange: 1 small*
Orange juice: 1/2 cup*
Papaya: 1/3 medium*
Passionfruit: 1
Passionfruit juice: 1/3 cup
Peach: 1 medium
Pear: 1 small
Persimmon: 1/2 medium
Pineapple, fresh or canned without
    sugar: 1/2 cup
Pineapple juice: 1/3 cup
Plantain: 1/2 small
Plums: 2 medium
Pomegranate: 1 small
Prunes, fresh or dried: 2
Prune juice: 1/4 cup
Raisins: 2 tablespoons
Raspberries: 1/2 cup
Strawberries: 3/4 cup
Tangerines: 1 large or 2 small

  * good source of vitamin C
 ** good source of vitamin A
*** good source of vitamins A and C

VEGETABLE EXCHANGE LIST

Each portion below equals
1 Vegetable Exchange,
is equal to 1 cup unless
otherwise specified, and contains
approximately:
5 grams of carbohydrate
2 grams of protein
25 calories

Alfalfa sprouts †
Artichoke, whole, base and ends
    of leaves (1)
Asparagus †
Bean sprouts †
Beets (1/2 cup)
Beet greens †
Broccoli*** †
Brussels sprouts*
Cabbage* †
Carrots (medium, 1)**
Cauliflower †
Celery †
Celery root (1/2 cup)
Chard †
Chayote
Chicory** †
Chilies †
Cilantro †
Chives*** †
Collard* †
Cucumbers †
Dandelion greens †
Eggplant
Endive †

13

exchange lists

Escarole** †
Green beans, mature (1/2 cup)
Green onion tops †
Jerusalem artichokes (1/2 cup)
Kale* †
Leeks (1/2 cup)
Lettuce †
Lima beans, baby (1/4 cup)
Mushrooms †
Mustard, fresh* †
Okra
Onions (1/2 cup)
Palm heart
Parsley*** †
Peas (1/2 cup)
Peppers, green and red* †
Poke †
Pumpkin (1/2 cup)*
Radishes †
Rhubarb †
Romaine lettuce †
Rutabagas (1/2 cup)
Spinach †
Squash, acorn (1/2 cup)
Squash, Hubbard (1/2 cup)
String beans
Summer squash †
Tomatoes
Tomato catsup (1-1/2 table-
    spoons)
Tomato juice (1/2 cup)
Tomato paste (3 tablespoons)
Tomato sauce (1/2 cup)
Turnips (1/2 cup)
V-8 juice (2/3 cup)**
Water chestnuts (medium, 4)

Watercress** †
Zucchini squash †

 * good source of vitamin C
 ** good source of vitamin A
 *** good source of vitamins A and C
 † calories negligible when eaten raw

BREAD EXCHANGE LIST

Each portion below equals
1 Bread Exchange and contains
approximately:
15 grams of carbohydrate
2 grams of protein
70 calories

VEGETABLES
Beans, dried, cooked (lima, soya,
    navy, kidney): 1/2 cup
Beans, baked, without pork: 1/4 cup
Corn, on-the-cob: 1 4 inches long
Corn, cooked and drained: 1/3 cup
Hominy: 1/2 cup
Lentils, dried, cooked: 1/2 cup
Parsnips: 1 small
Peas, dried, cooked, black-eyed,
    split: 1/2 cup
Poi: 1/2 cup
Potatoes, sweet, yams: 1/4 cup**
Potatoes, white, baked or boiled:
    1 2 inches in diameter
Potatoes, white, mashed: 1/2 cup
Potato chips: 15 2 inches in diameter
Pumpkin, canned: 1 cup
Rice, brown, cooked: 1/3 cup
Rice, white, cooked: 1/2 cup

Tomato catsup, commercial:
    3 tablespoons

BREADS
Bagel: 1/2
Biscuit: 1 2 inches in diameter
Bread, rye: 1 slice
Bread, whole wheat: 1 slice
Bread (white and sourdough): 1 slice
Breadsticks: 4 9 inches long
Bun, hamburger: 1/2
Bun, hot dog: 2/3
Corn bread: 1 piece 1-1/2 inches
    square
Cracked wheat (bulgur):
    1-1/2 tablespoons
Croutons, plain: 1/2 cup
English muffin: 1/2
Matzo cracker, plain:
    1 6 inches in diameter
Melba toast: 6 slices
Muffin, unsweetened:
    1 2 inches in diameter
Pancakes: 2 3 inches in diameter
Popover: 1
Roll: 1 2 inches in diameter
Rusks: 2
Spoon bread: 1/2 cup
Tortilla, corn, flour:
    1 7 inches in diameter
Waffle: 1 4 inches in diameter

CEREALS
All-Bran: 1/2 cup
Bran Flakes: 1/2 cup
Bran, unprocessed rice: 1/3 cup
Bran, unprocessed wheat: 1/3 cup

Cheerios: 1 cup
Concentrate: 1/4 cup
Corn flakes: 2/3 cup
Cornmeal, cooked: 1/2 cup
Cream-of-Wheat, cooked: 1/2 cup
Grapenuts: 1/4 cup
Grapenut Flakes: 1/2 cup
Grits, cooked: 1/2 cup
Kix: 3/4 cup
Life: 1/2 cup
Malt-O-Meal, cooked: 1/2 cup
Maypo, cooked: 1/2 cup
Matzo meal, cooked: 1/2 cup
Oatmeal, cooked: 1/2 cup
Pep: 1/2 cup
Puffed rice: 1-1/2 cups

FLOURS

Arrowroot: 2 tablespoons
All-purpose: 2-1/2 tablespoons
Bisquick: 1-1/2 tablespoons
Bran, unprocessed wheat:
　　5 tablespoons
Buckwheat: 3 tablespoons
Cake: 2-1/2 tablespoons
Cornmeal: 3 tablespoons
Cornstarch: 2 tablespoons
Matzo meal: 3 tablespoons
Potato flour: 2-1/2 tablespoons
Rye, dark: 4 tablespoons
Whole wheat: 3 tablespoons
Noodles, macaroni, spaghetti,
　　cooked: 1/2 cup
Noodles, dry, egg: 3-1/2 ounces
Noodles, cooked, egg:
　　3-1/2 ounces

CRACKERS

Animal: 8
Arrowroot: 3
Cheese tidbits: 3/4 cup
Graham: 2
Oyster: 20 or 1/2 cup
Pretzels: 10 very thin, or 1 large
Saltines: 5
Soda: 3
Ritz: 6
RyKrisp: 3
Rye thins: 10
Triangle thins: 14
Triscuits: 5
Vegetable thins: 12
Wheat thins: 12

MISCELLANEOUS

Cocoa, dry, unsweetened:
　　2-1/2 tablespoons
Ice cream, low-saturated: 1/2 cup
Popcorn, popped, unbuttered:
　　1-1/2 cups
Potato chips, Fritos: 3/4 ounce or
　　1/2 cup

LOW-FAT MEAT EXCHANGE LIST

Each portion below equals 1 Low-fat Meat Exchange and contains approximately:
7 grams of protein
3 grams of fat
55 calories

CHEESE

Cottage cheese, low-fat: 1/4 cup
Farmer: 1/4 cup, crumbled
Hoop: 1/4 cup
Pot: 1/4 cup
Ricotta, part skim: 1/4 cup or
　　2 ounces

EGG SUBSTITUTES

Liquid egg substitute: 1/4 cup
Dry egg substitute: 3 tablespoons

CHICKEN

Broiled or roasted: 1 ounce or
　　1 slice 3 x 2 x 1/8 inches
Breast, without skin: 1/2 small,
　　1 ounce or 1/4 cup, chopped
Leg: 1/2 medium or 1 ounce

TURKEY

Meat, without skin: 1 ounce or
　　1 slice 3 x 2 x 1/8 inches

OTHER POULTRY AND GAME

Buffalo: 1 ounce or 1 slice
　　3 x 2 x 1/8 inches
Cornish game hen, without skin:
　　1/4 bird or 1 ounce
Pheasant: 1-1/2 ounces
Rabbit: 1 ounce or 1 slice
　　3 x 2 x 1/8 inches
Quail, without skin: 1/4 bird or
　　1 ounce
Squab, without skin: 1/4 bird or
　　1 ounce
Venison, lean, roast or steak:
　　1 ounce or 1 slice 3 x 2 x 1/8 inches

15

exchange lists

FISH AND SEAFOOD
Abalone: 1-1/3 ounces
Albacore, canned in oil: 1 ounce
Anchovy fillets: 9
Bass: 1-1/2 ounces
Caviar: 1 ounce
Clams, fresh: 3 large or 1-1/2 ounces
Clams, canned: 1-1/2 ounces
Clam juice: 1-1/2 cups
Cod: 1 ounce
Crab, canned: 1/2 ounce
Crab, cracked, fresh: 1-1/2 ounces
Flounder: 1-2/3 ounces
Frog legs: 2 large or 3 ounces
Halibut: 1 ounce or 1 piece
   2 x 2 x 1 inches
Herring, pickled: 1-1/4 ounces
Lobster, fresh: 1-1/2 ounces,
   1/4 cup or 1/4 small lobster
Lobster, canned: 1-1/2 ounces
Oysters, fresh: 3 medium or
   1-1/2 ounces
Oysters, canned: 1-1/2 ounces
Perch: 1-1/2 ounces
Red snapper: 1-1/2 ounces
Salmon: 1 ounce
Salmon, canned: 1-1/2 ounces
Sand dabs: 1-1/2 ounces
Sardines: 4 small
Scallops: 3 medium or 1-1/2 ounces
Sole: 1-2/3 ounces
Shrimp, fresh: 5 medium
Shrimp, canned: 5 medium or
   1-1/2 ounces
Swordfish: 1-1/2 ounces
Trout: 1-1/2 ounces
Tuna: 1 ounce

Tuna, canned: 1/4 cup
Turbot: 1-1/2 ounces

BEEF
Flank steak: 1-1/2 ounces
Rib roast: 1 ounce, 1/4 cup, chopped,
   or 1 slice 3 x 2 x 1/8 inches
Steak, very lean (filet mignon, New
   York, sirloin, T-bone): 1 ounce or
   1 slice 3 x 2 x 1/8 inches
Tripe: 1 ounce or 1 piece 5 x 2 inches

LAMB
Chops, lean: 1/2 small chop or 1 ounce
Roast, lean: 1 ounce, 1 slice 3 x 2 x
   1/8 inches or 1/4 cup, chopped

PORK
Ham: 1 ounce or 1 slice 3 x 2 x
   1/8 inches

VEAL
Chop: 1/2 small or 1 ounce
Cutlet: 1 ounce or 1 slice
   3 x 2 x 1/8 inches
Roast: 1 ounce or 1 slice
   3 x 2 x 1/8 inches

MEDIUM-FAT MEAT EXCHANGE LIST

Each portion below equals
1 Medium-fat Meat Exchange and
contains approximately:
7 grams of protein
5 grams of fat
75 calories

CHEESE
Cottage cheese, creamed: 1/4 cup
Feta: 1 ounce
Mozzarella: 1 ounce
Parmesan: 1/4 cup, 2/3 ounce or
   4 tablespoons
Ricotta, regular: 1/4 cup or 2 ounces
Romano: 1/4 cup, 2/3 ounce or
   4 tablespoons

EGGS
Eggs, medium: 1

CHICKEN
Heart: 1 ounce
Liver: 1 ounce

BEEF
Brains: 1 ounce
Corned beef, canned: 1 ounce or
   1 slice 3 x 2 x 1/8 inches
Hamburger, very lean (4 ounces raw =
   3 ounces cooked): 1 ounce
Heart: 1 ounce or 1 slice 3 x 2 x 1/8
   inches
Kidney: 1 ounce or 1 slice
   3 x 2 x 1/8 inches
Liver: 1 ounce or 1 slice 3 x 2 x 1/8
   inches
Tongue: 1 slice 3 x 2 x 1/4 inches

PORK
Canadian bacon: 1 slice 2-1/2 inches
   in diameter, 1/4 inch thick
Chops, lean: 1/2 small chop or
   1 ounce

Liver: 1 ounce
Roast, lean: 1 ounce, 1 slice
   3 x 2 x 1/8 inches or 1/4 cup,
   chopped

VEAL

Calves' liver: 1 ounce or 1 slice
   3 x 2 x 1/8 inches
Sweetbreads: 1 ounce, 1/4 pair or
   1/4 cup, chopped

HIGH-FAT MEAT EXCHANGE LIST

Each portion below equals 1 High-
fat Meat Exchange and contains
approximately:
7 grams of protein
7 grams of fat
95 calories

CHEESE

American: 1 ounce
Bleu: 1 ounce or 1/4 cup,
   crumbled
Cheddar: 1 ounce
Edam: 1 ounce
Liederkranz: 1 ounce
Monterey Jack: 1 ounce
Muenster: 1 ounce
Pimiento cheese spread: 1 ounce
Roquefort: 1 ounce or 1/4 cup,
   crumbled
Stilton: 1 ounce or 1/4 cup, crumbled
Swiss: 1 ounce

COLD CUTS

Bologna: 1 ounce or 1 slice
   4-1/2 inches in diameter,
   1/8 inch thick
Liverwurst: 1 slice 3 inches in
   diameter, 1/4 inch thick
Spam: 1 ounce
Salami: 1 ounce or 1 slice 4 inches in
   diameter, 1/3 inch thick
Vienna sausage: 2-1/2 sausages or
   1 ounce

DUCK

Roasted, without skin: 1 ounce or
   1 slice 3 x 2 x 1/8 inches
Wild duck, without skin: 1/4 small

BEEF

Brisket: 1 ounce
Frankfurters: 1 (8 to 9 per pound)
Short ribs, very lean: 1 rib or 1 ounce

PEANUT BUTTER

Peanut butter: 2 tablespoons

PORK

Bacon (see Fat Exchange List)
Sausage: 2 small or 1 ounce
Spareribs, without fat: meat from
   3 medium or 1 ounce

FAT EXCHANGE LIST

Each portion below equals 1 Fat
Exchange and contains
approximately:
5 grams of fat
45 calories

Avocado: 1/8 4 inches in diameter
Bacon, crisp: 1 slice
Butter: 1 teaspoon
Caraway seeds: 2 tablespoons
Cardamom seeds: 2 tablespoons
Chocolate, bitter: 1/3 ounce or
   1/3 square
Cream cheese: 1 tablespoon
Cream, light, coffee: 2 tablespoons
Cream, heavy, whipping: 1 tablespoon
Cream, half-and-half: 3 tablespoons
Cream, sour: 2 tablespoons
Cream, sour, imitation: 2 tablespoons
   (Imo, Matey)
Margarine, polyunsaturated:
   1 teaspoon
Mayonnaise: 1 teaspoon
Oils, polyunsaturated: 1 teaspoon
Olives: 5 small
Poppy seeds, 1-1/2 tablespoons
Pumpkin seeds, 1-1/2 teaspoons
Salad dressings, commercial
   French oil and vinegar
      1-1/2 teaspoons
   Roquefort: 1 teaspoon
   Thousand Island (egg-free):
      1 teaspoon
Sauces, commercial
   Béarnaise: 1 teaspoon
   Hollandaise: 1 teaspoon
   Tartar sauce: 1 teaspoon
Sesame seeds: 2 teaspoons
Sunflower seeds: 1-1/4 teaspoons

NUTS

Almonds: 7
Brazil nuts: 2

exchange lists

Cashews: 7
Coconut, fresh: 1 piece 1 x 1 x
   3/8 inches
Coconut, shredded, unsweetened:
   2 tablespoons
Filberts: 5
Hazelnuts: 5
Hickory nuts: 7 small
Macadamia nuts: 2
Peanuts, Spanish: 20
Peanuts, Virginia: 10
Pecans: 6 halves
Pine nuts: 1 tablespoon
Pistachio nuts: 15
Soy nuts, toasted: 3 tablespoons
Walnuts, black: 5 halves
Walnuts, California: 5 halves

NON-FAT MILK EXCHANGE LIST

Each portion below equals
1 Non-fat Milk Exchange
and contains approximately:
12 grams of carbohydrate
8 grams of protein
trace of fat
80 calories

Milk, powdered, skim: 1/4 cup
Milk, skim, non-fat: 1 cup
Milk, evaporated, skim: 1/2 cup
Buttermilk: 1 cup
Yogurt, plain, non-fat: 1 cup

LOW-FAT MILK EXCHANGE LIST

Each portion below equals
1 Low-fat Milk Exchange
and contains approximately:
12 grams of carbohydrate
8 grams of protein
5 grams of fat
125 calories

Milk, low-fat, 2% fat: 1 cup
Yogurt, plain, low-fat: 1 cup

WHOLE MILK EXCHANGE LIST

Each portion below equals 1 Whole
Milk Exchange and contains
approximately:
12 grams of carbohydrate
8 grams of protein
10 grams of fat
170 calories

Milk, whole: 1 cup
Milk, evaporated, whole: 1/2 cup
Yogurt, plain, whole: 1 cup
Ice milk: 1 cup

FREE FOODS LIST!!!

Calories are negligible and need not be
counted in the following list. An
excess of many of these foods, however, is not good for you.

Coffee
Tea
Clear broth
Consommé and bouillon (fat-free)
Gelatin (unsweetened)
Rennet Tablets
Cranberries (unsweetened)
Mustard
Mint
Pickles (without sugar)
Herbs
Spices
Extracts
Angostura bitters
Soy sauce
Vinegar
Lemon
Some vegetables, uncooked,
   see pages 13 and 14

MEASURING FOOD

Most foods you eat must be measured. You will need: a standard 8-ounce measuring cup, a set of measuring spoons, a ruler and a tape measure. It is also handy to have a small food scale. It makes it easier to find the measured amounts of foods you usually purchase by weight, for example cheese. Be sure that all measurements are level and remember that most foods should be measured after cooking.

PREPARING YOUR FOOD

Meats, fish and poultry should be baked, broiled or boiled. Do not fry foods unless you are using only the amount of fat allowed on your diet for that day. Your vegetables may be prepared with those for other members of your family. Your portion should be removed before extra fat or flour is added unless you are calculating the amounts and using only what is allowed on your diet.

EAT ONLY THOSE FOODS WHICH ARE ON YOUR EXCHANGE LISTS.

EAT ONLY THE AMOUNTS OF FOODS ON YOUR DIET PROGRAM.

DO NOT SKIP MEALS.

DO NOT EAT BETWEEN ALLOWED MEALS.

YOUR DOCTOR WILL PRESCRIBE THE CORRECT EXCHANGE DIET PROGRAM FOR YOU.

FOODS TO AVOID

Sugar
Candy
Honey
Jam
Jelly
Marmalade
Syrups
Pie
Cake
Cookies
Pastries
Condensed milk, sweetened
Soft drinks
Gum, sweetened with sugar
Beer, wine or other alcoholic beverages (except with the consent and supervision of your doctor)
Fried, scalloped or creamed foods

alcoholic beverages

CALORIE AND CARBOHYDRATE ALCOHOLIC BEVERAGES CHART

Ale, mild, 8 oz. = 98 C*, 8 GC**
Beer, 8 oz. = 114 C, 11 GC

WINES

Champagne brut, 3 oz. = 75 C, 1 GC
Champagne, extra dry, 3 oz.=87 C, 4 GC
Dubonnet, 3 oz. = 96 C, 7 GC
Dry Marsala, 3 oz. = 162 C, 18 GC
Sweet Marsala, 3 oz. = 182 C, 23 GC
Muscatel, 4 oz. = 158 C, 14 GC
Port, 4 oz. = 158 C, 14 GC
Red wine, dry, 3 oz. = 69 C, under 1 GC
Sake, 3 oz. = 75 C, 6 GC
Sherry, domestic, 3½ oz. = 84 C, 5 GC
Dry vermouth, 3½ oz. = 105 C, 1 GC
Sweet vermouth, 3½ oz. = 167 C, 12 GC
White wine, dry, 3 oz.=74 C, under 1 GC

LIQUEURS AND CORDIALS (BOLS)

Creme de Cacao, 1 oz. = 101 C, 12 GC
Creme de Menthe, 1 oz. = 112 C, 13 GC
Curacao, 1 oz. = 100 C, 9 GC
Drambuie, 1 oz. = 110 C, 11 GC
Tia Maria, 1 oz. = 113 C, 9 GC

SPIRITS

Bourbon, brandy, Cognac, Canadian whiskey, gin, rye, rum, scotch, tequila and vodka are all carbohydrate free! The calories they contain depend upon the proof.
80 proof, 1 oz. = 67 C
84 proof, 1 oz. = 70 C
90 proof, 1 oz. = 75 C
94 proof, 1 oz. = 78 C
97 proof, 1 oz. = 81 C   *C = calories
100 proof, 1 oz. = 83 C   **GC = Grams of Carbohydrates

Most doctors allow small amounts of alcoholic beverages. Dry table wine contains so little carbohydrate that it is negligible. The caloric content of a 3-ounce glass of dry red wine is 69 and there are 74 calories in a 3-ounce glass of dry white wine. Bourbon, Scotch, rye, rum, gin, vodka and cognac contain no carbohydrates. You will find a complete calorie and carbohydrate chart for most alcoholic beverages on this page. Usually if a doctor allows any drinking at all, he will limit it either to a drink before dinner or a glass or two of wine with dinner. Not both! Your doctor will determine how the alcohol is to be computed in your diet.

Insulin is not required to assimilate alcohol. However, alcohol does affect your judgement. Therefore a one-drink-before-dinner limit is a good rule to follow. After two or three martinis, a diabetic is much more apt to eat "forbidden foods" than without the martinis. Also, eating on a regular time schedule is important for proper control of diabetes and an extended cocktail hour can postpone dinner much too long.

I feel about saving up my drinks for wine with my meals just like I do about saving up my Fat Exchanges for more dressing on my salads. I would rather never have a drink before dinner than give up wine with my dinner, and I would never have butter on my toast at breakfast if I have to eat "too dry" salads in exchange for it. However, there are those who covet that one Scotch before dinner and wouldn't give it up for any wine in the world.

Most doctors consider cooking with wines completely acceptable. Wine adds so little food value to each portion and all of the alcohol is cooked away before the food is eaten.

MENU PLANNING

At first we all have trouble planning menus so that all the exact amounts of everything we are supposed to be eating come out right (that is called an understatement!).

The biggest problem is that it is impossible to get away from using fractions, parts of Exchanges, in recipes. To make this problem as simple as possible I have kept all of the fractions the same throughout the book. They are all either 1/4, 1/2 or 3/4 of the whole Exchange portion.

An easy way to plan your menus is to always think of each Exchange as looking like this

 1 EXCHANGE

Then as you use each part of the Exchange think of it like this:

1/4 EXCHANGE · 3/4 LEFT

1/2 EXCHANGE · 1/2 LEFT

3/4 EXCHANGE · 1/4 LEFT

For example you may have 1/4 of a Bread Exchange in your main dish. So think of it like this

1/4 EXCHANGE · 3/4 LEFT

Isn't it easier to picture 3/4 of a slice of bread or 3/4 of 1/2 cup of rice this way?! Or go a step further and use another 1/2 Bread Exchange in your salad (croutons). You had this

1/4 EXCHANGE · 3/4 LEFT

now you have

3/4 EXCHANGE · 1/4 LEFT

No need to fret over how to use 1/4 Bread Exchange in a gourmet fashion. Just eat 2 tablespoons of rice or 1/4 slice of bread and forget it.

If you learn to keep this mental picture, even going through a cafeteria line will cease to be a nightmare. You first pick up a salad with 1/4 cup pineapple

1/2 FRUIT EXCHANGE

1/2 FRUIT EXCHANGE LEFT

and 1/2 cup of low-fat cottage cheese

 2 LOW-FAT MEAT EXCHANGES

Now you don't have any more Meat Exchanges left because you only have 2 for that meal, but you still have

1/2 FRUIT EXCHANGE · 1 BREAD EXCHANGE

1/2 MILK EXCHANGE LEFT

Then you see 1/4 cup blueberries. Great, now your Fruit Exchange looks like this

Just like it should!

Take 1/2 pint of milk, pour 1/2 of it over your blueberries

Take 2 graham crackers

eat them with your blueberries and milk for dessert. You've had a perfectly balanced lunch.

Start using the menu programs beginning on page 22 as a guide. Look at all of them for ideas, not just the ones for your calorie level. Before long you will have fun planning your own menus easily and with imagination.

sample menus

3 DAY MENU FOR
800 CALORIES PER DAY

2 Milk Exchanges (Subtract 1 Fat
Exchange for each Low-fat Milk
Exchange and 2 Fat Exchanges
for each Whole Milk Exchange)
3 Meat Exchanges (Subtract 1/2 Fat
Exchange for each Medium-fat
Meat Exchange and 1 Fat Exchange
for each High-fat Meat Exchange)
2 Bread Exchanges
2 Fruit Exchanges
2 Vegetable Exchanges
2 Fat Exchanges

FIRST DAY
Breakfast
1 slice FRENCH TOAST (1 Medium-fat Meat Exchange, 1 Bread
Exchange), page 97
1/2 serving CITRUS SAUCE COM-
POTE, page 163 (3/4 Fruit
Exchange)
1/2 cup non-fat milk (1/2 Non-fat
Milk Exchange)

Lunch
SOUFFLÉ TEXTURED TUNA
ASPIC, page 90, on lettuce bed
(2 Low-fat Meat Exchanges)
1-1/2 teaspoons MAYONNAISE
DRESSING, page 61 (1/2 Fat
Exchange)

1/4 cup fresh watermelon (1/4 Fruit
Exchange)
1 cup non-fat milk (1 Non-fat Milk
Exchange)

Dinner
GARDEN SALAD, page 76, with
dressing (1-1/4 Fat Exchanges)
1 ounce ham (1 Low-fat Meat
Exchange)
1 fresh peach, sliced (1 Fruit Exchange)
1/2 cup WHIPPED MILK TOPPING,
page 72, made with non-fat milk
on top of the peach
(1/2 Non-fat Milk Exchange)

SECOND DAY
Breakfast
1/2 cup oatmeal (1 Bread Exchange)
with
2 tablespoons raisins (1 Fruit
Exchange) and
1 cup non-fat milk (1 Non-fat Milk
Exchange)

Lunch
1/4 cup grated Parmesan cheese
(1 Medium-fat Meat Exchange)
on a lettuce salad made with
1 teaspoon ITALIAN DRESSING,
page 63 (1/2 Fat Exchange)
1 cup non-fat milk (1 Non-fat Milk
Exchange)

Dinner
Salad with 1/4 cup chopped cold
beets, with lemon juice (1/2
Vegetable Exchange)
COQ AU VIN, page 134 (2 Low-fat
Meat Exchanges, 1/2 Fat Ex-
change, 1/2 Vegetable Exchange)
1/2 cup TOASTED PILAF, page 156
(1 Bread Exchange)
1 PARTY PEAR IN SAUTERNE
SAUCE, page 162 (2 Fruit
Exchanges, 1/2 Fat Exchange)

THIRD DAY
Breakfast
2 MY PANCAKES, page 144
(1 Bread Exchange)
6 tablespoons STRAWBERRY JAM,
page 73 (1/4 Fruit Exchange)
1 cup non-fat milk (1 Non-fat Milk
Exchange)

Lunch
SPINACH SALAD, page 79 (1 Fat
Exchange) with
1 ounce shredded chicken breast
meat (1 Low-fat Meat Exchange)
3 slices melba toast (1/2 Bread
Exchange)
1/4 cup applesauce (1/2 Fruit
Exchange) with
1/2 cup WHIPPED MILK TOPPING,
page 72, made with non-fat milk
(1/2 Non-fat Milk Exchange)
DESERT TEA, page 179

Dinner

2 ounces HOT POACHED SALMON,
page 105 (2 Low-fat Meat
Exchanges)

1/2 serving COLD PEA SALAD, page
79 (1/2 Vegetable Exchange, 1-1/4
Fat Exchanges)

1/2 slice ONION-DILL BREAD, page
141 (1/2 Bread Exchange)

2 servings PINEAPPLE WHIP,
page 165, made with non-fat milk
(1 Fruit Exchange, 1/2 Non-fat
Milk Exchange)

Undertake 800 calories per day only
under supervision of a physician.

3 DAY MENU FOR
1000 CALORIES PER DAY

2 Milk Exchanges (Subtract 1 Fat
Exchange for each Low-fat Milk
Exchange and 2 Fat Exchanges
for each Whole Milk Exchange)

5 Meat Exchanges (Subtract 1/2 Fat
Exchange for each Medium-fat
Meat Exchange and 1 Fat Exchange
for each High-fat Meat Exchange)

2 Bread Exchanges

3 Fruit Exchanges

2 Vegetable Exchanges

2 Fat Exchanges

FIRST DAY
Breakfast

1/2 cup fresh orange juice
(1 Fruit Exchange)

1 POACHED EGG, page 94 (1 Medium-fat Meat Exchange) on

1 slice wheat toast (1 Bread Exchange)

1 cup non-fat milk
(1 Non-fat Milk Exchange)

Lunch

OYSTER STEW SOUP, page 50
(1/2 Low-fat Meat Exchange,
1/4 Low-fat Milk Exchange, 1/2
Vegetable Exchange, 1/4 Bread
Exchange, 1 Fat Exchange)

GARDEN SALAD, page 76,
(1-1/4 Fat Exchanges)

2 servings PINEAPPLE WHIP, page
165, made with low-fat milk
(1 Fruit Exchange, 1/2 Low-fat
Milk Exchange)

Dinner

1/2 carrot in sticks and
cold assorted, raw vegetables
(1/2 Vegetable Exchange)

COLD CHICKEN CONSOMMÉ,
page 41

3 ounces RAPID ROAST LAMB,
page 118 (3 Low-fat Meat
Exchanges)

1/2 cup TOASTED PILAF, page
156 (1 Bread Exchange)

SEMI-TROPICAL FRUIT CUP,
page 167 (1 Fruit Exchange)

SECOND DAY
Breakfast

1/2 baked grapefruit (1 Fruit
Exchange)

1 slice (1 ounce) boiled ham on

1 slice wheat bread (1 Medium-fat
Meat Exchange, 1 Bread Exchange)

1 cup non-fat milk
(1 Non-fat Milk Exchange)

Lunch

Lettuce salad with

1/4 cup shrimp,

1/3 chopped papaya and

1-1/2 teaspoons CURRY DRESSING,
page 65 (1 Low-fat Meat Exchange,
1 Fruit Exchange, 1/2 Fat Exchange)

1 slice whole wheat bread
(1 Bread Exchange)

1 cup WHIPPED MILK TOPPING,
page 72, made with non-fat milk,
and sprinkled with cinnamon
(1 Non-fat Milk Exchange)

Dinner

Cold, assorted raw vegetables

CHICKEN JEANNO, page 137
(3 Medium-fat Meat Exchanges,
1-1/2 Fat Exchanges)

Baked zuchinni (1 Vegetable
Exchange)

Chilled grapes (1 Fruit Exchange)

sample menus

THIRD DAY

Breakfast

3/4 cup puffed wheat (1/2 Bread
    Exchange)
EGG & MILK CEREAL TOPPING,
    page 74 (1 Medium-fat Meat
    Exchange, 1 Low-fat Milk
    Exchange, 1/4 Fruit Exchange)
3/4 cup fresh strawberries on
    cereal (1 Fruit Exchange)

Lunch

ANTIPASTO SALAD, page 83 (1 High-
    fat Meat Exchange, 1/4 Bread
    Exchange, 2 Fat Exchanges)
1 slice French bread (1 Bread
    Exchange)
1/8 chilled cantaloupe (1/2 Fruit
    Exchange)
1/2 cup non-fat milk (1/2 Non-fat
    Milk Exchange)

Dinner

Raw vegetables and 1/4 cup non-fat
    yogurt (1/4 Non-fat Milk Exchange)
3 ounces STEAK AU POIVRE, page
    119 (3 Low-fat Meat Exchanges)
1/2 cup peas and onions (1 Vegetable
    Exchange)
CITRUS SAUCE COMPOTE, page
    163 with
1/2 cup WHIPPED MILK TOPPING,
    page 72, made with non-fat milk
    (1-1/4 Fruit Exchanges, 1/2 Non-
    fat Milk Exchange)

3 DAY MENU FOR
1200 CALORIES PER DAY

2 Milk Exchanges (Subtract 1 Fat
    Exchange for each Low-fat Milk
    Exchange and 2 Fat Exchanges
    for each Whole Milk Exchange)
5 Meat Exchanges (Subtract 1/2 Fat
    Exchange for each Medium-fat
    Meat Exchange and 1 Fat Exchange
    for each High-fat Meat Exchange)
4 Bread Exchanges
3 Fruit Exchanges
2 Vegetable Exchanges
3 Fat Exchanges

FIRST DAY

Breakfast

1 slice FRENCH TOAST, page 97
    (1 Medium-fat Meat Exchange,
    1 Bread Exchange)
1/2 serving CITRUS SAUCE COM-
    POTE, page 163 (1/2 Fruit
    Exchange)
1/2 cup non-fat milk (1/2 Non-fat
    Milk Exchange)

Lunch

Sliced tomatoes (1/2 Vegetable
    Exchange)
2 ounces ham, thinly sliced (2
    Low-fat Meat Exchanges) on
2 slices rye bread spread with
    mustard (2 Bread Exchanges)
1/2 CINNAMON BAKED APPLE,
    page 160 (1 Fruit Exchange) with:
1/2 cup WHIPPED BUTTERMILK
    TOPPING, page 72 (1/2 Non-fat
    Milk Exchange)

Dinner

Consommé
CARROT SALAD, page 77 (1 Vege-
    table Exchange, 1/2 Fruit Ex-
    change, 1 Fat Exchange)
1/2 serving SALMON LOAF, page 110
    (1-1/4 Low-fat Meat Exchanges)
6 tablespoons rice (3/4 Bread
    Exchange)
1 cup broccoli with 3 tablespoons
    HAPPY HOLLANDAISE SAUCE,
    page 60 (1 Vegetable Exchange,
    1/4 Medium-fat Meat Exchange,
    1/4 Bread Exchange, 3/4 Fat
    Exchange)
1 cup INSTANT CUSTARD TOP-
    PING, page 72, made with non-fat
    milk (1 Non-fat Milk Exchange,
    1/2 Medium-fat Meat Exchange,
    1/4 Fruit Exchange) over 1 sliced
    peach (1 Fruit Exchange)

SECOND DAY
Breakfast
1/2 cup oatmeal (1 Bread Exchange) mixed with
1 tablespoon raisins (1/2 Fruit Exchange) and
1/4 cup low-fat cottage cheese (1 Low-fat Meat Exchange)
1/2 cup non-fat milk on oatmeal (1/2 Non-fat Milk Exchange)
1/2 cup non-fat milk to drink (1/2 Non-fat Milk Exchange)

Lunch
1-1/2 servings SOUFFLÉ TEXTURED BEEF ASPIC, page 91 (3 Low-fat Meat Exchanges)
1/2 cup cold pickled beets (1 Vegetable Exchange)
1-3/4 slices hot ONION-DILL BREAD, page 141 (1-3/4 Bread Exchanges)
1/2 orange, sliced (1/2 Fruit Exchange)
1 cup non-fat milk (1 Non-fat Milk Exchange)

Dinner
ANTIPASTO SALAD, page 83 (1 High-fat Meat Exchange, 1/4 Bread Exchange, 2 Fat Exchanges)
1 slice French bread (1 Bread Exchange)
1 PARTY PEAR IN SAUTERNE SAUCE, page 162 (2 Fruit Exchanges, 1/2 Fat Exchange)

THIRD DAY
Breakfast
1/4 cantaloupe (1 Fruit Exchange)
1 POPOVER, page 145 (1 Bread Exchange)
1 ounce ham (1 Low-fat Meat Exchange)
1 cup non-fat milk (1 Non-fat Milk Exchange)

Lunch
OYSTERS FLORENTINE, page 114 (1-1/2 Low-fat Meat Exchanges, 3/4 Fat Exchange, 1/2 Whole Milk Exchange, 1/4 Bread Exchange)
6 tablespoons TOASTED PILAF, page 156 (3/4 Bread Exchange)
1/2 BUTTERMILK BAKED TOMATO, page 154 (1 Vegetable Exchange)
1/3 papaya with lime (1 Fruit Exchange)

Dinner
Celery and carrot sticks (1 Vegetable Exchange)
2-1/2 ounces liver (2-1/2 Medium-fat Meat Exchanges) with
1/2 cup onions (1 Vegetable Exchange)

2 potato pancakes (1 Bread Exchange)
3/4 cup fresh strawberries (1 Fruit Exchange) with
1/2 cup WHIPPED MILK TOPPING, page 72, made with low-fat milk (1/2 Low-fat Milk Exchange)

3 DAY MENU FOR 1500 CALORIES PER DAY

2 Milk Exchanges (Subtract 1 Fat Exchange for each Low-fat Milk Exchange and 2 Fat Exchanges for each Whole Milk Exchange)
6 Meat Exchanges (Subtract 1/2 Fat Exchange for each Medium-fat Meat Exchange and 1 Fat Exchange for each High-fat Meat Exchange)
5 Bread Exchanges
4 Fruit Exchanges
2 Vegetable Exchanges
6 Fat Exchanges

FIRST DAY
Breakfast
1/2 baked grapefruit (1 Fruit Exchange)
EGGS BENEDICT, page 95 (2 Medium-fat Meat Exchanges, 1-1/4 Bread Exchanges, 3/4 Fat Exchange)
1 cup non-fat milk (1 Non-fat Milk Exchange)

sample menus

Lunch

2 servings CURRIED CRAB CRÊPES, page 108 (1/2 Whole Milk Exchange, 2 Low-fat Meat Exchanges, 1-1/2 Bread Exchanges, 2 Fat Exchanges)

1 PARTY PEAR IN SAUTERNE SAUCE, page 162 (2 Fruit Exchanges, 1/2 Fat Exchange)

1 slice BANANA BREAD, page 142 (1 Bread Exchange, 1/4 Fruit Exchange, 1 Fat Exchange)

Dinner

CORNED BEEF AND CABBAGE, page 127 (2 Medium-fat Meat Exchanges) with

1/2 cup carrots (1 Vegetable Exchange)

1/4 cup potatoes (1 Bread Exchange)

1 slice RYE BREAD, page 141 (1 Bread Exchange)

1/2 BAKED CINNAMON APPLE, page 160 with

1/2 cup WHIPPED MILK TOPPING, page 72, made with low-fat milk (1 Fruit Exchange, 1/2 Low-fat Milk Exchange)

SECOND DAY

Breakfast

1 PUFFY PANCAKE, page 144 (1 Medium-fat Meat Exchange, 1/4 Bread Exchange)

1 teaspoon butter (1 Fat Exchange)

CITRUS SAUCE COMPOTE, page 163 (1-1/4 Fruit Exchanges)

1 cup non-fat milk (1 Non-fat Milk Exchange)

Lunch

SPINACH SALAD, page 79, without eggs (1 Fat Exchange)

SOUFFLÉ TEXTURED HAM ASPIC, page 91 (1-1/2 Low-fat Meat Exchanges, 1/4 Bread Exchange)

3 slices ONION-DILL BREAD, page 141 (3 Bread Exchanges)

3/4 cup blackberries with

1/2 cup WHIPPED MILK TOPPING, page 72 (3/4 Fruit Exchange, 1/2 Whole Milk Exchange)

Dinner

GARDEN SALAD, page 76 (1-1/4 Fat Exchanges)

Broiled steak (3 Low-fat Meat Exchanges)

STUFFED MUSHROOMS, page 154 (1/2 Bread Exchange, 1/2 Fat Exchange, 1/4 Medium-fat Meat Exchange)

1/2 cup steamed green peas (1 Vegetable Exchange)

1 small baked potato (1 Bread Exchange)

MANGO WHIP, page 164 (1/4 Low-fat Milk Exchange, 1 Fruit Exchange)

1 graham cracker (1/2 Bread Exchange)

THIRD DAY

Breakfast

1/2 cup cooked oatmeal with cinnamon and

2 dates chopped in oatmeal (1 Bread Exchange, 1 Fruit Exchange)

1 ounce ham (1 Low-fat Meat Exchange)

Hot chocolate made with 1 cup non-fat milk, 1/3 ounce bitter chocolate and 3/4 teaspoon fructose (1 Non-fat Milk Exchange, 1 Fat Exchange, 1/4 Fruit Exchange)

Lunch

Lettuce salad with 2 teaspoons FRENCH DRESSING, page 62 (1 Fat Exchange)

REAL FRENCH ONION SOUP, page 44 (2 High-fat Meat Exchanges, 1 Vegetable Exchange, 1 Bread Exchange, 1 Fat Exchange)

1 slice French bread (1 Bread Exchange)

2 medium peaches, sliced (2 Fruit Exchanges)

Dinner

Sliced tomatoes (1/2 Vegetable
Exchange)
2-3/4 ounces RAPID ROAST, page
118 (2-3/4 Low-fat Meat Exchanges)
1 cup asparagus with 3 tablespoons
HAPPY HOLLANDAISE SAUCE,
page 60 (1 Vegetable Exchange,
1/4 Medium-fat Meat Exchange,
1/4 Bread Exchange, 3/4 Fat
Exchange)
1/2 cup mashed potatoes with
SKINNY BEEF GRAVY, page 53
(1 Bread Exchange)
1-inch cube sponge cake with 1/2
cup STRAWBERRY JAM, page
73 (1/2 Fruit Exchange, 3/4
Bread Exchange)
1 cup non-fat milk (1 Non-fat Milk
Exchange)

3 DAY MENU FOR
1800 CALORIES PER DAY

2-1/2 Milk Exchanges (Subtract 1 Fat
Exchange for each Low-fat Milk
Exchange and 2 Fat Exchanges
for each Whole Milk Exchange)
7 Meat Exchanges (Subtract 1/2 Fat
Exchange for each Medium-fat
Meat Exchange and 1 Fat Exchange
for each High-fat Meat Exchange)
6 Bread Exchanges
5 Fruit Exchanges
3 Vegetable Exchanges
7-1/2 Fat Exchanges

FIRST DAY
Breakfast
2 WAFFLES, page 146 (2 Bread
Exchanges)
2 servings CITRUS SAUCE COM-
POTE, page 163 (2-1/2 Fruit
Exchanges)
2 ounces ham (2 Low-fat Meat
Exchanges)
1 cup non-fat milk (1 Non-fat Milk
Exchange)

Lunch
1 artichoke (1 Vegetable Exchange)
1 tablespoon MAYONNAISE DRESS-
ING, page 61 (1 Fat Exchange)
FONDUE SOUFFLÉ, page 100 (1/2
Whole Milk Exchange, 2 High-fat
Meat Exchanges, 1 Bread Exchange)
3/4 cup raspberries with
1/2 cup WHIPPED MILK TOPPING,
Page 72 (1-1/2 Fruit Exchanges,
1/2 Whole Milk Exchange)
2 graham crackers (1 Bread Exchange)

Dinner

EGG FLOWER SOUP, page 47 (1/2
Medium-fat Meat Exchange)
SWEET AND SOUR PORK, page
124 (2-1/2 Medium-fat Meat Exchanges, 1 Vegetable Exchange,
1 Fat Exchange)
1 cup steamed rice (2 Bread
Exchanges)
SEMI-TROPICAL FRUIT CUP, page
167 (1 Fruit Exchange)
1/2 cup whole milk (1/2 Whole Milk
Exchange)

SECOND DAY
Breakfast
2 egg OMELETTE, page 102, with
1 cup STRAWBERRY JAM FILL-
ING, page 73 (2 Medium-fat Meat
Exchanges, 1-1/2 Fruit Exchanges)
1 English muffin (2 Bread Exchanges)
1-1/2 teaspoons butter (1-1/2 Fat
Exchanges)
1 cup non-fat milk (1 Non-fat
Milk Exchange)

Lunch
CHICKEN SALAD, page 88 (2 Low-fat
Meat Exchanges, 3/4 Fruit
Exchange, 2-1/4 Fat Exchanges)
1/2 cup carrot sticks (1 Vegetable
Exchange)
6 rye crackers (2 Bread Exchanges)
1-1/2 servings PEACH WHIP, page
165 (1/4 Low-fat Milk Exchange,
3/4 Fruit Exchange)

sample menus

Dinner

GARDEN SALAD, page 76 (1-1/4 Fat Exchanges)

JONES STEW, page 122 (2 Low-fat Meat Exchanges, 1 Vegetable Exchange, 1/2 Fat Exchange, 1/4 Bread Exchange)

1-3/4 servings SPOON BREAD, page 148 (1-3/4 Bread Exchanges, 1/2 Medium-fat Meat Exchange)

1 ounce cheddar cheese (1 High-fat Meat Exchange)

1 large apple (2 Fruit Exchanges)

1-1/4 cups low-fat milk (1-1/4 Low-fat Milk Exchanges)

THIRD DAY

Breakfast

1 cup orange juice (2 Fruit Exchanges)

1 cup cream of wheat (2 Bread Exchanges)

2 tablespoons raisins (1 Fruit Exchange)

1 ounce Canadian bacon (1 Medium-fat Meat Exchange)

1 cup non-fat milk (1 Non-fat Milk Exchange)

Lunch

COLE SLAW, page 84 (1 Fat Exchange)

2 servings EGGPLANT NEPTUNE, page 116 (2 Low-fat Meat Exchanges, 2 Vegetable Exchanges, 1 Fat Exchange)

1/2 BUTTERMILK BAKED TOMATO, page 154 (1 Vegetable Exchange)

2 slices ONION-DILL BREAD, page 141 (2 Bread Exchanges)

3/4 cup strawberries (1 Fruit Exchange)

1 cup whole milk (1 Whole Milk Exchange)

Dinner

MONTEREY JACK CHEESE SOUP, page 46 (1/2 Low-fat Milk Exchange, 1 High-fat Meat Exchange, 1/4 Fat Exchange)

Sandwich with 3 ounces of lean beef (3 Low-fat Meat Exchanges, 2 Bread Exchanges) and

2-1/2 teaspoons mayonnaise (2-1/2 Fat Exchanges)

1 medium nectarine (1 Fruit Exchange)

3 DAY MENU FOR 2100 CALORIES PER DAY

2-1/2 Milk Exchanges (Subtract 1 Fat Exchange for each Low-fat Milk Exchange and 2 Fat Exchanges for each Whole Milk Exchange)

8 Meat Exchanges (Subtract 1/2 Fat Exchange for each Medium-fat Meat Exchange and 1 Fat Exchange for each High-fat Meat Exchange)

7-1/2 Bread Exchanges

6 Fruit Exchanges

3 Vegetable Exchanges

9-1/2 Fat Exchanges

FIRST DAY

Breakfast

1 broiled grapefruit (2 Fruit Exchanges)

HUEVOS RANCHEROS, page 96 (2 Medium-fat Meat Exchanges, 1 Bread Exchange)

2 tortillas (2 Bread Exchanges)

1 teaspoon butter (1 Fat Exchange)

1 cup whole milk (1 Whole Milk Exchange)

Lunch

3-ounce ham sandwich with

1 tablespoon mayonnaise (3 Low-fat
    Meat Exchanges, 2 Bread Exchanges,
    Exchanges, 3 Fat Exchanges)

CARROT SALAD, page 77 (1 Vege-
    table Exchange, 1/2 Fruit Exchange,
    1 Fat Exchange)

2 fresh peaches with

1/2 cup WHIPPED MILK TOPPING,
    page 72 (2 Fruit Exchanges, 1/2
    Whole Milk Exchange)

Dinner

2/3 cup V-8 juice cocktail (1 Vege-
    table Exchange)

BEEF STROGANOFF, page 120
    (3 Low-fat Meat Exchanges,
    1-1/2 Fat Exchanges)

3/4 cup noodles (1-1/2 Bread
    Exchanges)

1/2 cup sweet and sour red cabbage
    (1/2 Vegetable Exchange)

1 slice RYE BREAD, page 141 (1
    Bread Exchange)

1/3 cantaloupe (1-1/2 Fruit Ex-
    changes)

1 cup non-fat Milk (1 Non-fat
    Milk Exchange)

SECOND DAY
Breakfast

1/2 cup orange juice (1 Fruit
    Exchange)

2 PUFFY PANCAKES, page 144
    (2 Medium-fat Meat Exchanges,
    1/2 Bread Exchange)

1 cup BOYSENBERRY JAM, page
    73 (1-1/2 Fruit Exchanges)

1 cup bran cereal (2 Bread
    Exchanges)

1 cup whole milk (1 Whole Milk
    Exchange)

Lunch

1/2 cup cold pickled beets
    (1 Vegetable Exchange)

4-1/2 ounces cold RAPID ROAST,
    page 118 (4-1/2 Low-fat Meat
    Exchanges)

SPINACH SALAD, page 79
    (1/4 Medium-fat Meat Exchange,
    1 Fat Exchange)

1-1/2 slices ONION-DILL BREAD,
    page 141 (1-1/2 Bread Exchanges)

SEMI-TROPICAL FRUIT CUP, page
    167 (1 Fruit Exchange)

1 cup whole milk (1 Whole Milk
    Exchange)

Dinner

2 servings CURRIED CRAB CRÊPES,
    page 108 (1/2 Whole Milk Ex-
    change, 2 Low-fat Meat Exchanges,
    1-1/2 Bread Exchanges, 2 Fat
    Exchanges)

Baked winter squash (1 Vegetable
    Exchange)

2 slices BANANA BREAD, page 142
    (2 Bread Exchanges, 1/2 Fruit Ex-
    change, 2 Fat Exchanges)

3/4 cup fresh pineapple (1-1/2 Fruit
    Exchanges)

Coffee or tea

THIRD DAY
Breakfast

3/4 cup apple juice (1-1/2 Fruit
    Exchanges)

1-1/2 cups oatmeal with 2 tablespoons
    cottage cheese and 1/2 teaspoon
    butter mixed in (1-1/2 Bread Ex-
    changes, 1/2 Low-fat Meat Ex-
    change, 1/2 Fat Exchange)

1/2 banana on cereal (1 Fruit
    Exchange)

1 ounce Canadian bacon (1 Medium-
    fat Meat Exchange)

1 cup non-fat milk (1 Non-fat Milk
    Exchange)

sample menus

Lunch
COLD PEA SALAD, page 79
(1 Vegetable Exchange, 2-1/2 Fat
Exchanges)
TURKEY SOUP, page 48 (2 Low-fat
Meat Exchanges, 1/2 Bread Ex-
change, 1 Fat Exchange)
12 Wheat Thins (1 Bread Exchange)
1/2 cup vanilla ice cream (1 Bread
Exchange, 2 Fat Exchanges)
1-1/2 cups strawberries (2 Fruit
Exchanges)
3/4 cup whole milk (3/4 Whole Milk
Exchange)

Dinner
GAZPACHO, page 51 (1 Vegetable
Exchange)
MARINATED GREEN BEANS, page
80 (1 Vegetable Exchange)
2 CHILIS RELLENOS WITH CHEESE
SAUCE, page 132 (1/2 Low-fat
Milk Exchange, 4-1/2 Low-fat Meat
Exchanges, 1/2 Fruit Exchange)
2 tortillas (2 Bread Exchanges)
2 teaspoons butter (2 Fat Exchanges)
MANGO WHIP, page 164 (1/4 Low-fat
Milk Exchange, 1 Fruit Exchange)

3 DAY MENU FOR 2500 CALORIES PER DAY

3 Milk Exchanges (Subtract 1 Fat
Exchange for each Low-fat Milk
Exchange and 2 Fat Exchanges
for each Whole Milk Exchange)
9 Meat Exchanges (Subtract 1/2 Fat
Exchange for each Medium-fat
Meat Exchange and 1 Fat Exchange
for each High-fat Meat Exchange)
10 Bread Exchanges
7 Fruit Exchanges
3 Vegetable Exchanges
11 Fat Exchanges

FIRST DAY
Breakfast
1 cup orange juice (2 Fruit
Exchanges)
3 pieces FRENCH TOAST, page 97
(3 Medium-fat Meat Exchanges,
3 Bread Exchanges)
3/4 cup STRAWBERRY JAM, page
73 (1-1/2 Fruit Exchanges)
1 teaspoon butter (1 Fat Exchange)
1 cup whole milk (1 Whole Milk
Exchange)

Lunch
TOSTADA with beets and carrots,
page 92 (1/2 Low-fat Milk Exchange, 3 Medium-fat Meat Exchanges, 1 Bread Exchange, 1-1/2
Vegetable Exchanges)
2 warm tortillas (2 Bread Exchanges)
1 cup fresh pineapple with
1/2 cup WHIPPED MILK TOPPING,
page 72 (1/2 Whole Milk Exchange, 2 Fruit Exchanges)

Dinner
1 artichoke (1 Vegetable Exchange)
2 tablespoons MAYONNAISE DRESS-
ING, page 61 (2 Fat Exchanges)
3 ounces broiled chicken (3 Low-
fat Meat Exchanges)
1/2 BUTTERMILK BAKED TOMATO,
page 154 (1 Vegetable Exchange)
1 cup TOASTED PILAF, page 156
2 Bread Exchanges
2 rolls (2 Bread Exchanges)
1 cup low-fat milk (1 Low-fat Milk
Exchange)
2/3 fresh papaya with lime (2 Fruit
Exchanges)

SECOND DAY
Breakfast
1 cup apple juice (2 Fruit Exchanges)
1 cup oatmeal (2 Bread Exchanges)
2 tablespoons raisins in oatmeal
    (1 Fruit Exchange)
1 cup whole milk (1 Whole Milk
    Exchange)
1/2 English muffin (1 Bread
    Exchange)
1 teaspoon butter (1 Fat Exchange)
2 ounces Canadian bacon
    (2 Medium-fat Meat Exchanges)

Lunch
2 cold roast beef sandwiches
    (3 ounces beef) with
2 teaspoons mayonnaise (3 Low-fat
    Meat Exchanges, 2 Fat Exchanges,
    4 Bread Exchanges)
MARINATED GREEN BEANS,
    page 80 (1 Vegetable Exchange)
GARDEN SALAD, page 76, with
3 tablespoons HORSERADISH DRESS-
    ING, page 60 (1/2 Fat Exchange)
1/2 cantaloupe with
1/2 cup vanilla ice cream (2 Fruit
    Exchanges, 1 Bread Exchange,
    2 Fat Exchanges)
1 cup low-fat milk (1 Low-fat Milk
    Exchange)

Dinner
1/3 recipe COLD CUCUMBERS IN
    DILL SAUCE, page 84 (1/2 Fruit
    Exchange)
3-1/2 ounces POACHED SALMON,
    page 105 (3-1/2 Low-fat Meat
    Exchanges) with
6 tablespoons HAPPY HOLLANDAISE
    SAUCE, page 60 (1/2 Medium-fat
    Meat Exchange, 1/2 Bread Ex-
    change, 1-1/2 Fat Exchanges)
1/2 cup green peas (1 Vegetable
    Exchange)
1-1/2 slices ONION-DILL BREAD,
    page 141 (1-1/2 Bread Exchanges)
2 servings MANGO WHIP, page 164
    (1/2 Low-fat Milk Exchange,
    2 Fruit Exchanges)
1/2 cup whole milk (1/2 Whole Milk
    Exchange)

THIRD DAY
Breakfast
1-1/2 cups fresh pineapple (3 Fruit
    Exchanges)
EGGS BENEDICT, page 95 (2 Med-
    ium-fat Meat Exchanges, 1-1/4
    Bread Exchanges, 3/4 Fat
    Exchange)
1/2 English muffin (1 Bread Exchange)
1 teaspoon butter (1 Fat Exchange)
1 cup non-fat milk (1 Non-fat Milk
    Exchange)

Lunch
2 servings TURKEY SOUP, page 48
    (4 Low-fat Meat Exchanges,
    1 Bread Exchange, 2 Fat Exchanges)
COLD PEA SALAD, page 79 (1 Vege-
    table Exchange, 2-1/2 Fat
    Exchanges)
2 slices toasted RYE BREAD, page
    141 (2 Bread Exchanges)
1 teaspoon butter (1 Fat Exchange)
2 peaches, sliced (2 Fruit Exchanges)
1 cup non-fat milk (1 Non-fat Milk
    Exchange)

Dinner
Lettuce and tomato salad with
2 tablespoons FRENCH DRESSING,
    page 62 (3 Fat Exchanges)
CHILE CON CARNE, page 129 (3
    Low-fat Meat Exchanges, 1 Vege-
    table Exchange)
2 servings SPOON BREAD, page 148
    (2 Bread Exchanges, 1/2 Medium-
    fat Meat Exchange)
2 servings SEMI-TROPICAL FRUIT
    CUP, page 167 (2 Fruit Exchanges)

Making your own stocks takes so little time and makes such a difference in the flavor of your sauces and gravies. Once you have started making your own stocks you will use commercial bouillons for "emergencies only" (that's when you don't have any more of your own stock in the freezer).

In these emergencies you will find that the powdered beef-stock base and chicken-stock base in jars are a much better substitute for the "real thing" than either bouillon cubes or canned bouillons.

In making your own stocks you can either take the French housewife's approach and save up meat and poultry scraps and bones or you can buy fresh bones and meat. I think it is a good idea to keep a couple of big plastic bags in the freezer for bones and meat, one for beef and veal and the other for poultry. Lamb, ham and pork bones are not good for making an all-purpose stock because their flavor is too strong.

If you are going to buy bones (or talk your butcher into saving them for you) get veal or beef bones with as much meat as possible. It is not necessary to have meat for making stocks. Just bones will do, but the stocks will have a much richer flavor if some meat is used.

Soup is served hot and cold, thick and thin, delicate and robust. It can be a very light first course or a hearty main dish. It has great latitude in the Exchange Diet because you can make a soup which is a Free Food and need not be counted at all, such as a clear consommé. Or, you can make soup which contains practically all of the exchanges allowed for the meal, such as REAL ONION SOUP.

Once you start making your own soups you will never go back to opening cans!

stocks bouillons consommes and soups

3 pounds beef or veal bones
1 pound meat (optional)
2 carrots, scraped and cut in pieces
2 stalks celery, without leaves
1 onion, cut in half
1 tomato, cut in half
3 whole garlic buds
2 parsley sprigs
2 whole cloves
1/4 teaspoon thyme
1/4 teaspoon marjoram
1 bay leaf
10 whole peppercorns
cold water to cover by 1 inch
1 teaspoon salt
defatted beef drippings you
   might have stored

Makes about 2-1/2 quarts (10 cups)
FREE FOOD, calories negligible

BEEF STOCK

In a large pot or soup kettle put the bones, and enough cold water to cover by 1 inch. Bring them to a boil. Simmer slowly for 5 minutes and remove any scum that forms on the top. Add the meat, vegetables and spices and enough more cold water to cover by 1 inch. Cover, leaving the lid ajar about 1 inch to allow the steam to escape. Simmer very slowly for at least 5 hours. 10 hours are even better if you are going to be around to turn off the heat!

When you are through cooking the stock allow it to come to room temperature. Put the stock in the refrigerator, uncovered, overnight. When the fat has hardened on the surface it can be easily removed. After removing every bit of fat, warm the stock until it becomes liquid. Strain the liquid and add salt to taste.

If the flavor of your stock is too weak you can boil it down to evaporate some more of the water and concentrate its strength for a stronger flavor. (I always do this.)

Store the stock in the freezer. I like to put some of it in 1-cup containers and some of it in ice-cube trays for individual servings. (2 ice cubes = 1/4 cup).

CHICKEN STOCK

Put the chicken parts, whole chicken if you are going to cook one, vegetables and spices in an 8- to 10-quart pot or soup kettle. Add cold water to cover by 1 inch. Bring slowly to a boil. Cover, leaving lid ajar about 1 inch to allow steam to escape. Simmer very slowly for 3 hours or until whole chicken is tender. Remove chicken and continue to simmer stock for 3 or 4 hours longer. Cool stock to room temperature and proceed exactly as you do for BEEF STOCK.

Cooking the stewing chicken is helpful in two ways. First, it adds flavor to the stock. And, secondly, it gives you a beautifully seasoned chicken for your dinner or many other dishes hot or cold. Try serving the stewed chicken with TEXAS DUMPLINGS and STEAMED MUSTARD GREENS.

3 pounds chicken parts, wings, backs, etc.
1 whole stewing chicken (optional)
2 carrots, scraped and cut in pieces
2 stalks celery, without leaves
1 onion, cut in half
2 whole garlic buds
1 bay leaf
1/4 teaspoon basil
8 whole peppercorns
1 teaspoon salt
cold water to cover by 1 inch
4-5 drops yellow food coloring, if desired

Makes about 2-1/2 quarts (10 cups)
FREE FOOD, calories negligible

BROWN STOCK

Preheat oven to 400°. Brown bones and meat for 1/2 hour. Add carrots, celery and onions and brown together for another 1/2 hour, or until a rich brown in color. (This first step of browning the bones, meat and vegetables is done for color rather than for flavor and may be eliminated if you are in a hurry.) Then add caramel color and a drop of red food coloring to BEEF STOCK (Preceding Recipe) for the desired color.)

Put the brown meat and vegetables in a large pot with all of the other ingredients and add cold water to cover by 1 inch. Cover, leaving the lid ajar about 1 inch to allow the steam to escape. Simmer very slowly for at least 5 hours and proceed exactly as you do for regular beef stock.

Same ingredients exactly as
BEEF STOCK

Makes about 2-1/2 quarts
FREE FOOD, calories negligible

1 turkey carcass
1 onion, cut in quarters
1 carrot, scraped, and cut in pieces
2 bay leaves
1/2 teaspoon basil
1/4 teaspoon thyme
1/4 teaspoon marjoram
1 teaspoon salt
8 whole peppercorns
de-fatted turkey drippings
    you have stored
cold water to cover by 1 inch

Makes about 1-1/2 to 2 quarts
FREE FOOD, calories negligible

TURKEY STOCK

Break up the turkey carcass and put it in a 8- to 10-quart pot or soup kettle. Add the vegetables and spices and cold water to cover by 1 inch. Cover, leaving the lid ajar about 1 inch to allow steam to escape. Simmer slowly for 4 hours. Cool to room temperature and proceed exactly as you do for BEEF STOCK, page 34.

TURKEY GIBLET STOCK

Put all ingredients in a large saucepan and simmer slowly for 3 hours. Cool and strain the liquid off of the giblets and vegetables. Put the stock in the refrigerator (or freezer if you don't want to serve it right away). Discard the vegetables and chop the giblets into small pieces, including the lean meat on the neck. Put the chopped giblets in the refrigerator until you are ready to use them. Take the fat off the giblet stock after it is cold enough to form a layer on the top.

Giblet stock is delicious served over rice. Add the giblets to the stock and make it a meal!

Giblet gravy is also divine over your Christmas turkey. The recipe is on page 54.

turkey neck
turkey giblets, heart, gizzard and liver
1 stalk celery, cut in pieces
1 onion, cut in quarters
1 whole garlic bud
1 bay leaf
1/4 teaspoon basil
1/8 teaspoon thyme
1/8 teaspoon marjoram
1 teaspoon salt
4 whole peppercorns
de-fatted turkey drippings
cold water to cover by 1 inch
Makes 1-1/2 to 2 quarts
FREE FOOD, calories negligible
1 cup chopped giblets =
   4 Low-fat Meat Exchanges

CHICKEN GIBLET STOCK

Proceed exactly as you do for TURKEY GIBLET STOCK.

2 or 3 chicken necks
giblets, hearts, gizzards and
   livers from 2 or 3 chickens
1 stalk celery, cut in pieces
1 carrot, scraped and cut in pieces
1 onion, cut in quarters
2 bay leaves
1/4 teaspoon basil
1 teaspoon salt
4 whole peppercorns
cold water to cover by 1 inch

1 cup chopped giblets =
   4 Low-fat Meat Exchanges

4 cups water
1/4 cup white vinegar
1/2 lemon, sliced
1 celery stalk, sliced
1 carrot, sliced
1/2 onion, sliced
1 garlic bud, whole
1 bay leaf
6 peppercorns, whole
1-1/2 teaspoons salt

Makes 1 quart
FREE FOOD, calories negligible

2-1/2 quarts water
2 pounds fish heads, bones and
    trimmings
2 onions, sliced
5 parsley sprigs
1 carrot, sliced
1/2 teaspoon marjoram
4 whole peppercorns
1 teaspoon salt
1 tablespoon lemon juice

Makes 2 quarts (8 cups)
FREE FOOD, calories negligible

COURT BOUILLON

Any time you are going to cook shrimp, crab or lobster . . . or poach any fish, prepare a court bouillon first. Of course you can use fish stock for poaching fish but this court bouillon is much faster and easier to make and completely satisfactory. You just cannot compare seafood cooked in plain, old salty water to the seafood cooked in court bouillon.

Always be careful not to overcook seafood because overcooking makes it tough. For example: when cooking shrimp never allow them to boil more than 2 minutes. Cool them in the court bouillon.

Combine all of the above ingredients and cook for 45 minutes. This may be made ahead and it may be used many times. After each use store it in the freezer.

FISH STOCK

Bring all of the ingredients to a boil and simmer for 40 minutes. Line a collander or strainer with damp cheesecloth and strain the fish stock through it. Cool and keep refrigerated. If you are not planning to use the fish stock for 2 days or more, put it in the freezer.

BEEF CONSOMMÉ
(Clarified Beef Stock)

If you are going to serve consommé hot or cold you want it beautifully clear (imagine serving cloudy consommé!)

Beat the egg whites with a wire whisk until they are slightly foamy. Add 1 cup of the cold stock to the egg whites and beat lightly together. Put the other 3 cups of stock in a very clean saucepan with the other ingredients. (It is not necessary to add the other ingredients, but the consommé will have a much better flavor if you do!) Bring the stock to a boil and remove from the heat. Slowly pour the egg white and stock mixture into the stock, stirring with the wire whisk as you do. Put the saucepan back on a very low heat and mix gently until it starts to simmer. Put the pan half on the heat and half off so that it is barely simmering. Turn the pan around every few minutes. Simmer for 40 minutes.

Line a colander or a strainer with 2 or 3 layers of damp cheese-cloth. Gently ladle the consommé through the cheesecloth. Allow it to drain undisturbed until it has all seeped through.

Optional: Add 2 tablespoons Madeira if you are serving it hot and 2 tablespoons sherry if you are going to serve it cold.

If you are planning to serve the consommé cold and want it firm or if you are going to use it for aspics or molded salad, add 1 envelope of unflavored gelatin dissolved in 1/4 cup of cold water to the consommé while still hot.

4 cups BEEF STOCK , page 34
2 egg whites
3 tablespoons lean ground beef
1/2 teaspoon chervil
1 parsley sprig
2 green onion tops, chopped
1 carrot, chopped
salt to taste
2 tablespoons Madeira or sherry
1 envelope unflavored gelatin
   (optional)

Makes 4 cups
FREE FOOD, calories negligible

2 cups BEEF CONSOMMÉ
1 tablespoon Madeira
1/2 cup fresh mushrooms

Makes 4 servings
FREE FOOD, calories negligible

2 cups BEEF CONSOMMÉ, cold
1 tablespoon sherry
4 thin slices lemon
2 teaspoons fresh, minced parsley

Makes 4 servings
FREE FOOD, calories negligible

HOT BEEF CONSOMMÉ

Slice mushrooms thinly and broil under low heat for a few minutes. Heat consommé, add mushrooms and Madeira just before serving.

COLD BEEF CONSOMMÉ

Mix the sherry with the consommé and put in chilled cups or icers. Put a slice of lemon on top of each serving and sprinkle with minced parsley.

CHICKEN CONSOMMÉ
(Clarified Chicken Stock)

Proceed exactly as you do for BEEF CONSOMMÉ.

4 cups CHICKEN STOCK with
   all fat removed
2 egg whites
1 bay leaf
1 parsley sprig
2 green onion tops, chopped
1 carrot, chopped
salt to taste
1 envelope unflavored
   gelatin (optional)

Makes 4 cups
FREE FOOD, calories negligible

2 cups CHICKEN CONSOMMÉ
4 thin slices lemon
2 teaspoons fresh minced parsley

Makes 4 servings
FREE FOOD, calories negligible

HOT CHICKEN CONSOMMÉ

Place a slice of lemon on top of each cup of consommé and sprinkle the top with fresh, minced parsley.

2 cups CHICKEN CONSOMMÉ, cold
1 medium carrot, scraped and grated
1 green onion top, minced
1 hard-boiled egg, chopped
1/2 teaspoon lemon juice
4 teaspoons fresh, minced parsley

Makes 4 servings
Each serving contains:
    1/4 Vegetable Exchange
    1/4 Medium-fat Meat Exchange
    25 calories

COLD CHICKEN CONSOMMÉ

Mix consommé with grated carrots, minced green onion tops, chopped hard boiled egg and lemon juice. Put in 4 chilled cups or icers and sprinkle top with parsley.

CONSOMMÉ MADRILENE

Place all ingredients in a large pot or soup kettle except the gelatin and 1/4 cup of cold water. Cover, leaving the lid ajar about 1 inch to allow the steam to escape. Simmer for 2 hours. Soften gelatin in 1/4 cup water and add to hot consommé. Stir until completely dissolved. Cool slightly and strain through a fine strainer. Season to taste with salt and pepper. Add 2 drops of red food coloring, if desired, for better color! Cool to room temperature and refrigerate. When consommé is completely jelled, unmold and cut off the part containing the sediment. Cut up the clear part and serve in sherbet glasses or cups.

3 large, ripe tomatoes, sliced
2 stalks celery, chopped
1 leek, white part only, chopped
1 carrot, sliced
1 onion, sliced
1 teaspoon lemon juice
6 peppercorns
2 quarts (8 cups) CHICKEN STOCK
2 bay leaves
2 envelopes unflavored gelatin
1/4 cup cold water + 2 drops
    red food coloring (optional)

Makes 1 to 1-1/2 quarts
FREE FOOD, calories negligible

COLD CONSOMMÉ WITH MUSHROOMS

Pour lemon juice over thinly sliced mushrooms and put them in the refrigerator for at least 2 hours. Add the sliced mushrooms and the lemon juice to the 2 cups of cold consommé and mix well. Put the consommé in 4 chilled bowls or icers. Put 1 tablespoon of sour cream on top of each one. Put 1-1/4 teaspoons of caviar on top of each spoonful of sour cream.

2 cups CONSOMMÉ MADRILENE or
    BEEF CONSOMMÉ, cold
1 cup fresh thinly sliced mushrooms
1/4 cup fresh lemon juice
4 tablespoons sour cream*
5 teaspoons caviar

Makes 4 servings
Each serving contains:
    1/2 Fat Exchange
    1/4 Medium-fat Meat Exchange
    41 calories

*You can use yogurt to save the
    Fat Exchange!

stocks/soups

1 part CHICKEN STOCK, page 35
  or BEEF STOCK, page 34
1 part water

Bouillons are FREE FOODS,
  calories negligible

4 cups BEEF STOCK, page 34
2 large onions sliced very thinly,
  vertically (rather than across)
4 teaspoons butter
1/4 cup dry white wine
1/2 teaspoon freshly ground black
  pepper
salt to taste
4 slices dry French bread
2 cups grated Swiss cheese

Makes 4 servings
Each serving contains:
  1 Vegetable Exchange
  1 Fat Exchange
  1 Bread Exchange
  2 High-fat Meat Exchanges
  330 calories

CHICKEN AND BEEF BOUILLON

Put the stock and water in a pan and bring to a boil. Simmer for at least 15 minutes before using.

Bouillons are basically just weak stocks. For this reason I find it troublesome and confusing to actually make both stocks and bouillons from scratch. Troublesome, because I think the bouillon made from a good rich stock has a better flavor than most other bouillons, and confusing because I have enough trouble keeping track of everything in my freezer as it is.

Bouillon is fabulous for cooking vegetables, as it adds so much flavor and no food value!

REAL FRENCH ONION SOUP

Carefully slice each slice of French bread into 2 very thin slices. Put the bread in a 300° oven to dry it for about 5 minutes.

Melt the 2 teaspoons of butter in a heavy iron skillet. Put the 2 sliced onions in the pan and cook, covered, over very low heat until they are soft. Then take the lid off and turn the heat up to high. Brown the onions, stirring constantly so that they don't burn. When they are browned turn the heat back down and add the 1/4 cup of wine. Cook until the wine is almost absorbed. Add the pepper, salt and BEEF STOCK. Mix together well and simmer for 5 minutes.

Pour the soup into 4 oven-proof bowls. Place 2 thin slices of French bread on top of each bowl of soup. Allow to stand until the bread is saturated with soup and has expanded. Sprinkle 1/2 cup of grated Swiss cheese over each serving. Bake at 325° and cook 30 to 40 minutes or until the cheese is slightly browned.

If you wish to hold the soup for a few minutes leave it in the oven and turn the temperature to the lowest point possible.

CREAM OF CHEESE SOUP

Melt butter and add minced onion. Cover and cook until onion is clear and tender. Add flour and cook, stirring constantly, for 3 minutes. Remove from heat and add boiling milk all at once, stirring constantly with a wire whisk. Return to heat and add the boiling CHICKEN STOCK, page 35. Simmer slowly for 30 minutes, stirring occasionally to prevent scorching. Add all the other ingredients and cook until cheese is completely melted.

1 tablespoon butter
2 tablespoons minced onion
3-3/4 tablespoons all-purpose flour, sifted
3 cups whole milk, boiling
1 cup CHICKEN STOCK, page 35, boiling
1/2 teaspoon salt
1/4 teaspoon dry mustard
1/2 teaspoon Worcestershire sauce
1/8 teaspoon white pepper
1 drop Tabasco sauce
2 cups grated mild cheddar cheese

Makes 6 servings
Each serving contains:
    1/2 Fat Exchange
    1/4 Bread Exchange
    1/2 Whole Milk Exchange
    1-1/2 High-fat Meat Exchanges
    269 calories

1/2 cup finely chopped onion
1 large, ripe tomato, peeled and diced
2 large green chilis, veins and seeds
   removed, chopped
1/2 bud garlic minced
1 cup CHICKEN STOCK, page 35
1-1/2 cups WHITE SAUCE, page 55
1-1/2 cups low-fat milk
1/4 teaspoon salt
dash freshly ground black pepper
1-1/2 cups grated Monterey Jack
   cheese

Makes 6 servings
Each serving contains:
   1/4 Fat Exchange
   1/2 Low-fat Milk Exchange
   1 High-fat Meat Exchange
   169 calories

MONTEREY JACK CHEESE SOUP

Put the chopped onion, diced tomato, chopped chilis and garlic in a saucepan with 1 cup CHICKEN STOCK and simmer until the vegetables are tender. Slowly stir in WHITE SAUCE, page 55, stirring constantly. Add the milk slowly. Add salt, pepper and cheese. Simmer until the cheese melts.

Serve immediately because the cheese will coagulate if kept too long.

Serve with TOASTED TORTILLA TRIANGLES and a green salad.

EGG FLOWER SOUP

Bring the CHICKEN STOCK to a boil. Beat the eggs until they are frothy. Slowly pour the beaten eggs into the boiling CHICKEN STOCK. Stir constantly with a fork. Continue to stir the soup rapidly until the eggs are shredded and look like long strings. Serve very hot. Sprinkle the top of each bowl of soup with chopped green onion tops and put soy sauce on the table. A few drops in the soup are delicious.

3 cups CHICKEN STOCK, page 35
2 eggs
2 tablespoons chopped chives or
    green onion tops

Makes 4 servings
Each serving contains:
    1/2 Medium-fat Meat Exchange
    38 calories

2 quarts TURKEY STOCK, or 1 full
   recipe page 36, defatted and strained
2 teaspoons butter
2 tablespoons flour
1/4 cup rice, uncooked
1 stalk celery, finely chopped
4 more teaspoons butter
3 cups sliced fresh mushrooms
3 cups turkey meat, cooked and
   chopped
3 tablespoons Madeira

Makes 6 servings
Each serving contains:
   2 Low-fat Meat Exchanges
   1 Fat Exchange
   1/2 Bread Exchange
   190 calories

TURKEY SOUP

Put the TURKEY STOCK in a soup kettle and heat it to the boiling point. While the stock is heating melt 2 teaspoons of butter in a pan and add 2 tablespoons of flour. Cook the flour and butter for several minutes, stirring constantly. Do not allow it to brown. Slowly add about 2 cups of the hot stock to the flour mixture, stirring until it is completely blended. Pour the stock-flour mixture back into the pot containing the rest of the stock and add the uncooked rice and the celery. Simmer slowly for 30 minutes.

While the soup is simmering melt the additional 4 teaspoons of butter in a pan and cook the mushrooms in it until they are tender. Add the mushrooms and chopped turkey to the stock and simmer 30 minutes longer. Just before serving add 3 tablespoons of Madeira.

Variations: If I don't make TURKEY GRAVY then I put the defatted turkey drippings in the soup right along with the stock. I like it even better this way!

NEW ENGLAND CLAM CHOWDER

Put the chopped onion and the bacon bits in a hot, heavy iron skillet. Add a tablespoon of the clam juice from the canned clams. Cook until the onions are. clear. Transfer the onion mixture to a saucepan and add the diced potatoes. Pour all of the rest of the clam juice from the cans into the saucepan. Add chicken stock and cook until the potato is tender. Add the clams, milk, salt and pepper. Heat thoroughly and serve.

2 7-ounce cans chopped clams, plus
   all the liquid from the cans
2 onions, chopped
2 tablespoons imitation bacon bits
2 cups raw potato, diced and peeled
1 cup CHICKEN STOCK , page 35
2 cups low-fat milk
1/2 teaspoon salt
1/4 teaspoon white pepper

Makes 4 servings
Each serving contains:
   1 Low-fat Meat Exchange
   1 Bread Exchange
   1/2 Vegetable Exchange
   1/2 Low-fat Milk Exchange
   201 calories

1 pint (2 cups) oysters
2 cups minced onion
1 stalk celery, minced
2 garlic buds, minced
2 tablespoons minced parsley
6 cups CHICKEN STOCK , page 35
5 tablespoons flour
3 tablespoons butter
2 cups low-fat milk, warmed
1/4 teaspoon white pepper
salt to taste

Makes 8 servings
Each serving contains:
    1/2 Low-fat Meat Exchange
    1/2 Vegetable Exchange
    1/4 Low-fat Milk Exchange
    1/4 Bread Exchange
    1 Fat Exchange
    135 calories

OYSTER STEW-SOUP

Put 4 cups of chicken stock in a large pot or soup kettle. Add the minced onion, celery and garlic and boil slowly. Put 2 cups of CHICKEN STOCK in another saucepan with the oysters and bring to a boil for 3 minutes. After the oysters have boiled pour the stock, (not the oysters) into the pan with the vegetables and continue to boil slowly. Meanwhile chop half of the oysters.

Melt the butter and slowly add the flour. Cook the flour and butter for several minutes, being careful not to brown it. Slowly add the warmed milk. Stir constantly until the white sauce has thickened. Add the white pepper and the chopped oysters, reserving the whole ones. Slowly stir the white sauce into the vegetables and chicken stock. To this add the minced parsley and the remaining whole oysters.

This soup is even better if made the day before you plan to serve it; just reheat.

GAZPACHO
(Cold Mexican Soup)

Put 2 cups of tomato juice and all other ingredients except diced tomato, chives and lemon wedges in the blender. Blend until well mixed. Slowly add the remaining 2 cups of tomato juice to the blender. Pour the mixture into a large bowl and add the chopped tomato. Garnish with the chopped chives and serve with the lemon wedges.

Try serving this with TOASTED TORTILLA TRIANGLES!

4 cups tomato juice
1/2 onion, minced
1 small green bell pepper, minced
1/2 large cucumber, peeled and minced
2 canned green chilis, seeds removed
   and chopped
1-1/2 teaspoons Worcestershire sauce
1 garlic bud, minced
3/4 teaspoon Lawry's seasoned salt
1 drop Tabasco sauce (optional)
1/4 teaspoon freshly ground pepper
1 large tomato, finely diced
2 tablespoons chopped chives or
   green onion tops
2 lemons cut in wedges

Makes 8 servings
Each serving contains:
   1 Vegetable Exchange
   25 calories

gravies sauces and salad dressings

I feel like a sorcerer trying to make sauces taste like something they really aren't, but it is always worth the time. I have come up with some fabulous fakes, plus a few classics which are well worth saving up your Fat Exchanges all day to eat.

DEFATTED DRIPPINGS

If you love gravy but don't eat it because it's Fat, Fat, Fat, then one of your problems is solved. Just defat your drippings!

All drippings are defatted in the same manner. After cooking your roast beef, leg of lamb, chicken, turkey or whatever, remove it from the roasting pan and pour the drippings into a bowl. Put the bowl in the refrigerator until the drippings are cold and all of the fat has solidified on the top. Remove the fat and you have defatted drippings!

Now, if you are in a hurry for them because you want to serve your roast beef au jus with defatted drippings instead of "fat jus" then put the drippings in the freezer instead of the refrigerator. Put the roast in a warm oven to keep it from getting cold. After about 20 minutes you can remove the fat, heat the jus, and serve.

I always defat my drippings when I roast meat or poultry and keep them in the freezer. Defatted drippings add extra flavor to your stocks and are better than stocks for making the SKINNY GRAVIES on the following pages.

SKINNY BEEF GRAVY

Heat the DEFATTED DRIPPINGS in a saucepan. As soon as they become liquid, put a little of the liquid in a cup and add the cornstarch or arrowroot. Pour the arrowroot mixture back into the gravy. Add the optional ingredients if desired. Simmer until sauce thickens slightly.

BEEF STOCK can be stored in ice cube trays in the freezer and used for individual servings of this gravy: For one serving, use: 2 BEEF STOCK ice cubes, 1/4 teaspoon cornstarch or arrowroot, 1 teaspoon onion, chopped (optional).

1 cup DEFFATED BEEF
    DRIPPINGS, preceding page OR
1 cup concentrated beef stock
1 tablespoon cornstarch or arrowroot
2 drops caramel food coloring
2 drops red food coloring
Optional:
2 tablespoons minced onion,
    browned OR
1 tablespoon dehydrated onion
    flakes

FREE FOOD, calories negligible

sauces/dressings

1 cup DEFATTED CHICKEN
   DRIPPINGS, page 52
OR 1 cup concentrated chicken stock
1 tablespoon cornstarch or arrowroot
2 drops yellow food coloring
2 drops caramel food coloring
dash garlic powder (optional)

FREE FOOD, calories negligible

SKINNY CHICKEN GRAVY

Heat the DEFATTED DRIPPINGS in a saucepan. As soon as it becomes liquid, put a little of the liquid in a cup and add the cornstarch or arrowroot. Pour the arrowroot mixture back into the gravy. Add the optional ingredients, if desired. Simmer until it thickens slightly.

CHICKEN STOCK can be frozen in ice cube trays in the freezer and used for individual servings of this gravy. For one serving use 2 CHICKEN STOCK ice cubes, 1/4 teaspoon cornstarch or arrowroot, and 1 teaspoon chopped onion (optional).

2 cups DEFATTED TURKEY
   DRIPPINGS page 52
2 tablespoons cornstarch or arrowroot
1/2 cup minced green onion tops
   (optional)
1/2 cup chopped fresh
   mushrooms,(optional)
2 tablespoons minced parsley
   (optional)

FREE FOOD, calories negligible

SKINNY TURKEY GRAVY

Heat the DEFATTED DRIPPINGS in a saucepan. As soon as they become liquid, put a little of the liquid in a cup and add the cornstarch or arrowroot. Pour the arrowroot mixture back into the gravy. Add 1 or all of the optional ingredients if desired. Simmer until it thickens slightly.

2 cups DEFATTED GIBLET
   GRAVY page 37
same ingredients as for SKINNY
   TURKEY GRAVY
1 or 2 cups chopped giblet, page 37

Makes 4 servings as a main course
Each 1/4 cup chopped giblets:
   1 Low-fat Meat Exchange
   55 calories

SKINNY GIBLET GRAVY
(Chicken or Turkey)

Proceed exactly as you do for SKINNY TURKEY GRAVY. After adding the desired optional ingredients, add the chopped giblets. Simmer until well heated and slightly thickened.

I love this served over rice or bulghar (cracked wheat) as a main course.

MILK GLAZE
(For Poultry and Fish)

Heat the STOCK and milk together. Soften the gelatin in the cold water. Add the gelatin to the milk and STOCK. Add the salt and stir until the gelatin is dissolved completely. Do not boil! Cool slightly and pour over cold poultry or fish to glaze and decorate.

This recipe may easily be cut in half for smaller portions.

It is fun to glaze and decorate a whole, cold chicken or turkey for a buffet. Decorate it with fresh fruit or vegetables cut in fancy shapes. I also love cold POACHED SALMON done this way.

The amount of milk in each portion is so small that this glaze does not really need to be counted on the diet program!

1 cup STOCK (fish or chicken),
    pages 35 and 38
2 cups milk
2 envelopes unflavored gelatin
1/2 cup cold water
1/2 teaspoon salt

Calories negligible per serving

BASIC WHITE SAUCE

Put the milk in a saucepan on low heat. In another saucepan melt the butter and add the flour, stirring constantly. Cook the flour and butter for 3 minutes. Do not brown! Take the flour-butter mixture off of the heat and add the simmering milk all at once, stirring constantly with a wire whisk. Put the sauce back on low heat and cook slowly for 20 minutes, stirring occasionally. If you wish a thicker sauce, cook it for a little longer time. Add the salt. If there are lumps in the sauce (but there shouldn't be by this method), put it in the blender!

2 cups whole milk, boiling
1 tablespoon butter or corn oil
    margarine
2-1/2 tablespoons sifted flour
1/8 teaspoon salt

Makes 1-1/2 cups
Each 1/2 recipe (3/4 cup) contains:
    1-1/2 Fat Exchanges
    1/2 Bread Exchange
    1 Whole Milk Exchange
    271 calories
Each recipe (1-1/2 cups) contains:
    3 Fat Exchanges
    1 Bread Exchange
    2 Whole Milk Exchanges
    543 calories

1-1/2 cups BASIC WHITE SAUCE,
   preceding recipe
1/8 teaspoon white pepper
1/4 teaspoon dry mustard
1/2 cup grated sharp cheddar cheese

Makes 2 cups
1 cup contains:
   1-1/2 Fat Exchanges
   1/2 Bread Exchange
   1 Whole Milk Exchange
   1 High-fat Meat Exchange
   368 calories
1 recipe contains:
   3 Fat Exchanges
   1 Bread Exchange
   2 Whole Milk Exchanges
   2 High-fat Meat Exchanges
   735 calories

CHEDDAR CHEESE SAUCE

Heat 1 cup of BASIC WHITE SAUCE and add the pepper, dry mustard and grated cheese. Stir, over low heat, until the cheese is completely melted.

Variations: Add 1/2 cup of milk, if you want a thinner sauce, and add 1/2 Milk Exchange.

MORNAY SAUCE

Proceed exactly as you do for CHEDDAR CHEESE SAUCE.

Variations: When you are making CHICKEN MORNAY use 1/2 cup of CHICKEN STOCK, page 35 instead of 1/2 cup milk. When making a fish mornay, use FISH STOCK, page 38.

1-1/2 cups BASIC WHITE SAUCE,
 page 55
1/2 cup milk
1/2 cup grated Gruyère or
 Swiss cheese
1/8 teaspoon nutmeg
1/8 teaspoon white pepper

Makes 2 cups
Each cup contains:
 1-1/2 Fat Exchanges
 1/2 Bread Exchange
 1-1/4 Whole Milk Exchanges
 1 High-Fat Meat Exchange
 410 calories

2 eggs
1/2 cup cider vinegar
1/2 cup whole milk
3 tablespoons dry mustard
2 tablespoons butter or
    corn oil margarine
1/4 cup fructose

Makes 1-1/4 cups
Each recipe contains:
    2 Medium-fat Meat Exchanges
    6 Fat Exchanges
    1/2 Whole Milk Exchange
    4 Fruit Exchanges
    665 calories
5 tablespoons contain:
    1/2 Medium-fat Meat Exchange
    1-1/2 Fat Exchanges
    1 Fruit Exchange
    146 calories
2-1/2 tablespoons contain:
    1/4 Medium-fat Meat Exchange
    3/4 Fat Exchange
    1/2 Fruit Exchange
    73 calories

MUSTARD SAUCE

Beat eggs. Add vinegar, milk and dry mustard. Slowly bring to a boil, stirring constantly with a wire whisk. Continue stirring and allow to boil for 1 minute. Remove from heat and lump the 2 tablespoons of butter on the top. Allow to cool to room temperature. Add the fructose and stir in the butter. Store in the refrigerator. Excellent sauce for frankfurters, hot or cold ham, and even eggs.

TERIYAKI MARINADE

Use ground ginger only if you absolutely can't find the fresh. Using fresh ginger makes all the difference in the world in the taste; buy it when you can find it and keep it in the freezer sealed in a plastic bag.

Mix all ingredients together and store in the refrigerator for one day before using. Marinate chicken, beef or pork for 2 hours before broiling or barbequing over charcoal! Marinate fish and seafood for 1 hour before broiling. Try Teriyaki Lobster broiled over charcoal.

1-3/4 cups soy sauce
3 tablespoons fructose
2 buds garlic, crushed
1 tablespoon fresh ginger root, peeled and grated
or 1/2 teaspoon ground ginger

Each recipe contains:
   3 Fruit Exchanges
   120 calories

TARTAR SAUCE

Put the sour cream, mayonnaise, salt, lemon juice and pickle juice in the blender and blend until smooth.

Pour the mixture in a bowl and add onion, pickle and capers. Mix well and store in the refrigerator.

1 cup (1/2 pint) sour cream less 2 tablespoons
3 tablespoons mayonnaise
1/4 teaspoon salt
1 teaspoon lemon juice
2 teaspoons dill pickle juice
1 tablespoon minced onion
1 tablespoon chopped dill pickle
2 teaspoons capers

Each 1/2 cup contains:
   8 Fat Exchanges
   360 calories
1 tablespoon contains:
   1 Fat Exchange
   45 calories

sauces/dressings

2 tablespoons butter
1/4 cup sifted flour
1 cup boiling water
1/2 teaspoon salt
1/8 teaspoon white pepper
2 eggs, beaten
2 tablespoons freshly squeezed
   lemon juice
1/4 teaspoon Worcestershire sauce
dash cayenne pepper, optional
Makes 1-1/2 cups
Each recipe contains:
   6 Fat Exchanges
   2 Bread Exchanges (not quite)
   2 Medium-fat Meat Exchanges
   560 calories
3 tablespoons contain:
   3/4 Fat Exchange
   1/4 Bread Exchange
   1/4 Medium-fat Meat Exchange
   67 calories

1/2 cup JELLED MILK, made with
   buttermilk, page 66
1/2 cup cold buttermilk
1/2 cup sour cream
1/4 bud garlic, pressed
1/4 teaspoon salt
1 tablespoon horseradish

Makes 1-1/2 cups
3 tablespoons contain:
   1/2 Fat Exchange
   23 calories

HAPPY HOLLANDAISE SAUCE

Melt butter. Add flour and mix well. Cook, stirring constantly for 3 minutes. It is always important to cook flour or your sauces will taste like raw flour, but be careful not to brown the mixture. Add the boiling water all at once, stirring constantly with a wire whisk. When the mixture thickens remove from heat and very slowly add the beaten eggs, stirring constantly with the whisk. Add salt and white pepper. Return to low heat and cook for 1 minute, stirring constantly with the whisk. Remove from heat and stir in lemon juice and cayenne pepper.

I call this Happy Hollandaise Sauce because you don't have to worry as much about the Fat Exchanges as you do in regular hollandaise sauce.

Try this sauce on EGGS BENEDICT, EGGS TOLSTOY, asparagus, artichokes or cold cooked vegetables. Add a few capers and serve it with cold, poached salmon.

HORSERADISH DRESSING

Put all ingredients in the blender and blend until smooth.

MAGIC MAYONNAISE

Dip egg in boiling water for 30 seconds. Put the egg in the blender with the dry mustard, salt, lemon juice and 1/4 cup of the salad oil. Turn on low speed. Immediately start pouring in the remaining oil in a steady stream. Switch the blender to high speed for 3 or 4 seconds and then turn it off. I call this Magic Mayonnaise because in seconds, as if by magic, you have it! It's easy to make, delicious to eat and stores well in the refrigerator.

Variations: Add 1/4 garlic bud when serving the mayonnaise with cold seafood.

Substitute tarragon vinegar for the lemon juice as a sauce for vegetables. You can mix the tarragon vinegar mayonnaise with a little plain yogurt to make your Fat Exchange go farther!

1 raw egg at room temperature
1/4 teaspoon dry mustard
1/2 teaspoon salt
1 tablespoon lemon juice
1 cup salad oil

1 teaspoon contains:
   1 Fat Exchange
   45 calories

MAYONNAISE DRESSING

Put all ingredients in the blender and blend until smooth.

1 cup (1/2 pint) sour cream less
   2 tablespoons
3 tablespoons mayonnaise
1/4 teaspoon salt

Each 1/2 cup contains:
   8 Fat Exchanges
   360 calories
1 tablespoon contains:
   1 Fat Exchange
   45 calories

sauces/dressings

1-1/2 tablespoons wine vinegar
1 teaspoon lemon juice
1/4 teaspoon dry mustard
1/4 teaspoon salt
1 tablespoon water
5 tablespoons salad oil or olive oil
dash freshly ground black pepper
1/8 teaspoon basil OR tarragon,
   (optional)

Makes 1/2 cup
1 tablespoon contains:
   1-1/2 Fat Exchanges
   67 calories

FRENCH DRESSING

Mix the vinegar, lemon juice, mustard and salt until the salt is dissolved. Add the water. Slowly add the oil and mix thoroughly. Add the pepper and basil and pour the dressing into a jar with a tightly fitted lid. Shake vigorously for 30 seconds. Store in the refrigerator.

This recipe is for a small amount of dressing because French Dressing is much better when it is made the same day it is going to be used.

Variations: For some salads I like a little pressed fresh garlic. For marinating cold vegetables I add a dash (remember that's less than 1/8 teaspoon) celery seeds, too.

1 cup (1/2 pint) sour cream less
   2 tablespoons
3 tablespoons mayonnaise
5 flat filets of anchovies, drained
   and chopped
2 tablespoons tarragon vinegar
1 tablespoon red wine vinegar
1/2 cup minced parsley
1/4 cup chopped green onion tops
1/8 teaspoon salt
dash white pepper

Each 1/2 cup contains:
   8 Fat Exchanges
   360 calories
1 tablespoon contains:
   1 Fat Exchange
   45 calories

GREEN GODDESS DRESSING

Put all ingredients in the blender and blend until smooth and green!

ITALIAN DRESSING

Beat the vinegar, dry mustard, salt and fructose until the salt is dissolved. Add the wine and Worcestershire sauce. Mix the pepper, sweet basil, oregano and tarragon together well with a mortar and pestle. Add them to the dressing and mix well. Slowly add the oil and mix.

Place the dressing in a jar with a tightly fitted lid. Shake vigorously for 30 seconds. Chill before serving.

2 tablespoons red wine vinegar
1/2 teaspoon dry mustard
1 teaspoon salt
3/4 teaspoon fructose
1/4 cup dry red wine
1/2 teaspoon Worcestershire sauce
1/4 teaspoon black pepper, freshly
   ground
1/2 teaspoon sweet basil
1/2 teaspoon tarragon
1/4 teaspoon oregano
1/2 cup olive oil

Makes about 1 cup
1/2 cup contains:
   12 Fat Exchanges
   540 calories
1 tablespoon contains:
   1-1/2 Fat Exchanges
   67 calories

sauces/dressings

1 slice bacon, very crisp,
    cooled and blotted
1-1/2 tablespoons red wine vinegar
1/2 teaspoon hickory smoked salt
1/4 teaspoon dry mustard
dash black pepper, freshly ground
1 tablespoon water
5 tablespoons oil

1-1/2 teaspoon contains:
    1 Fat Exchange
    45 calories

1-1/2 tablespoons tarragon vinegar
1 teaspoon lemon
1/4 teaspoon dry mustard
1/2 teaspoon salt
3 tablespoons tomato juice
1/2 teaspoon grated onion
dash freshly ground black pepper
1/4 teaspoon fructose
1/8 teaspoon tarragon
5 tablespoons salad oil
1 bud garlic, quartered

Makes 1 generous cup
Each recipe contains:
    15 Fat Exchanges
    675 calories
1 tablespoon contains:
    1-1/2 Fat Exchanges
    67 calories

BACON DRESSING

Crumble the crisp bacon and add it to the vinegar in a jar with a tightly fitted lid. Add the hickory smoked salt, dry mustard and pepper. Mix until the salt is dissolved. Add the water and mix. Add the oil and shake vigorously for 30 seconds. Store in the refrigerator.

GARDEN SALAD DRESSING

Beat the vinegar, lemon juice, mustard and salt until the salt is dissolved. Add the tomato juice, onion, pepper, fructose and tarragon. Slowly add the oil and mix thoroughly. Add quartered garlic. Pour the dressing into a jar with a tightly fitted lid. Shake vigorously for 30 seconds. Store in the refrigerator.

CURRY DRESSING

Put all ingredients in the blender and blend until smooth.

1 cup (1/2 pint) sour cream less
   2 tablespoons
3 tablespoons mayonnaise
1/2 teaspoon curry powder
1/8 teaspoon powdered ginger
1/4 teaspoon salt

Each 1/2 cup contains:
   8 Fat Exchanges
   360 calories
1 tablespoon contains:
   1 Fat Exchange
   45 calories

sauces/dressings

1 envelope unflavored gelatin
1/4 cup water
1 cup milk (non-fat, low fat, whole
   or buttermilk may be used)

Makes 1 cup
1 cup made with non-fat milk
contains:
   1 Non-fat Milk Exchange
   80 calories
1 cup made with low-fat milk
contains:
   1 Low-fat Milk Exchange
   125 calories
1 cup made with whole milk
contains:
   1 Whole Milk Exchange
   170 calories

1/2 cup JELLED MILK, made with
   buttermilk, page 66
1/2 cup cold buttermilk
1/2 cup sour cream
1/4 teaspoon salt
1 tablespoon cider vinegar
1-1/2 teaspoons fructose
1/4 teaspoon dry mustard

Makes 1-1/2 cups
3 tablespoons contain:
   1/2 Fat Exchange
   23 calories

JELLED MILK

Put the water in a small saucepan. Sprinkle the gelatin on the top and allow it to soften. Place the saucepan on low heat, stirring constantly until the gelatin is completely dissolved. Do not allow it to come to a boil. Slowly pour the milk into the gelatin stirring as you do. Place the gelatin-milk mixture in the refrigerator. When it is jelled it is ready to use as JELLED MILK for many recipes.

JELLED MILK is used for TOSTADA TOPPING, ROQUEFORT DRESSING, WHIPPED MILK TOPPINGS, INSTANT CUSTARD, FRUIT WHIPS and many other things. It is a good idea to keep some in the refrigerator ready to use at any time!

Personally, I do not like the WHIPPED MILK TOPPINGS made with non-fat milk. However, I almost always use low-fat milk and I think it tastes just as good as whole milk and gives me one extra Fat Exchange!

COLE SLAW DRESSING

Put all ingredients in the blender and blend until smooth.

ROQUEFORT DRESSING

Put the JELLED BUTTERMILK and the cold buttermilk in the blender. Add the sour cream and all the other ingredients except 1 ounce of the roquefort cheese. Mix well. Pour dressing in a jar and add the remaining 1 ounce of roquefort cheese, crumbled. Make 24 hours before using and the flavor will be much better.

1/2 cup JELLED MILK, preceding
   recipe, made with buttermilk
1/2 cup cold buttermilk
1/2 cup sour cream
1/8 teaspoon garlic powder
1/4 teaspoon salt
1/4 cup grated Parmesan or
     Romano cheese
3 ounces Roquefort cheese

Makes about 2 cups
1/2 cup contains:
   1/4 Non-fat Milk Exchange
   1 Medium-fat Meat Exchange
   3 Fat Exchanges
   230 calories
2 tablespoons contain:
   1/4 Medium-fat Meat Exchange
   3/4 Fat Exchange
   53 calories

sauces/dressings

1 cup JELLED MILK, made with
   buttermilk, page 66
3/4 cup cold buttermilk
1/4 bud garlic
1/4 teaspoon Worcestershire sauce
1/4 teaspoon fructose
1 egg
1 tablespoon tarragon vinegar
1/2 teaspoon salt
1/8 teaspoon freshly ground
   black pepper
1/4 teaspoon tarragon

Makes 1-3/4 cups
Each recipe contains:
   1-3/4 Non-fat Milk Exchanges
   1 Medium-fat Meat Exchange
   215 calories
3 tablespoons contain:
   27 calories

CREAMY TARRAGON DRESSING

Put the JELLED BUTTERMILK and the buttermilk in the blender with the garlic, Worcestershire sauce and fructose and blend until liquid.

Put the egg, vinegar, salt, pepper and tarragon in the top of a double boiler, preferably one with a rounded bottom. Beat with a wire whisk until well mixed. Put over slowly boiling water and beat until it is thick. Remove from the heat.

Slowly pour the buttermilk mixture into the egg mixture stirring constantly. Refrigerate until thick and creamy.

CREAMY TOSTADA TOPPING

Drop the tomatoes into a saucepan of boiling water and cook for about 4 minutes, or until tomatoes can easily be pierced with a fork. Remove the peelings and core. Chop the chilis. Put all the ingredients in the blender. Blend until smooth. Chill until slightly thickened.

This is one recipe where I use powdered chicken stock base instead of my own chicken stock because the chicken stock base does not dilute the sauce.

Excellent topping for TOSTADAS with a little Parmesan cheese on top. I also use this recipe for salad dressing.

4 small green tomatoes (or 2 medium red tomatoes)
3 canned chilis with the seeds removed
1 cup low-fat JELLED MILK, page 66
1 cup cold low-fat milk
2 teaspoons powdered chicken stock base

Makes 4 cups
Each cup contains:
1/2 Low-fat Milk Exchange
63 calories

ONION-GARLIC DIP

Mix all ingredients together well. Put in the refrigerator for 24 hours before serving.

This is a divine dip for all raw vegetables. My favorites are: cauliflower divided into little flowerettes, zucchini cut in round slices, carrots cut in very thin curls, celery cut in thin sticks, little cherry tomatoes with the stems left on for handles, green bell peppers and red peppers, too, cut in strips, whole mushrooms with the stem ends cut short, radishes cut to look like flowers, turnips peeled and sliced very thin and cucumbers unpeeled and cut in round slices.

Variation: To cut Fat Exchanges in half, substitute 1/2 cup yogurt for 1/2 cup of the sour cream.

1 cup (1/2 pint) sour cream
1/4 teaspoon garlic powder
1 teaspoon onion powder
1/4 teaspoon dry mustard
dash fructose
1 teaspoon seasoned salt
1/4 teaspoon savory
1/4 teaspoon parsley flakes
2 drops Tabasco sauce

1 tablespoon contains:
1/2 Fat Exchange
23 calories

69

sauces/dressings

4 cups tomato juice
1/4 cup wine vinegar
2 buds garlic, whole
3/4 teaspoon fructose

Makes about 1-1/2 cups
2 tablespoons contain:
   1/4 Vegetable Exchange
   7 calories

TOMATO JUICE CATSUP

Put tomato juice, vinegar and garlic in a saucepan and bring to a boil. Reduce heat to very low and simmer for about 2-1/2 hours, or until desired thickness. Remove from heat and cool to room temperature. Remove garlic buds and add fructose. Store in the refrigerator in a glass or plastic container.

Now, if you are wondering why bother to fool around with tomato juice when you can buy perfectly good catsup in the store, I will tell you why I do it. One-half cup of tomato juice is only 1 Vegetable Exchange. Two tablespoons of commercial catsup is 1 Fruit Exchange or 3 tablespoons is 1 Bread Exchange. When you reduce 4 cups of tomato juice to 1-1/2 cups you get 3 tablespoons for only 1/4 Vegetable Exchange and 7 calories.

1 cup TOMATO JUICE CATSUP
   (preceding recipe)
1 tablespoon lemon juice
1 teaspoon horseradish or more

2 tablespoons contain:
   1/4 Vegetable Exchange
   7 calories

SEAFOOD COCKTAIL SAUCE

Mix together all ingredients and chill. Serve over cold, cooked shrimp, crab, lobsters or a combination of cold, cooked seafoods. I also like it on raw oysters and clams.

Variations: Add 2 tablespoons minced fresh parsley or 1/2 cup finely chopped celery.

1 cup TOMATO JUICE CATSUP,
   (preceding)
2 tablespoons lemon juice
1/4 cup minced raw onion
1/2 cup fresh minced cilantro

2 tablespoons contain:
   1/4 Vegetable Exchange
   7 calories

MARINARA COCKTAIL SAUCE

Mix all ingredients together and chill. Especially good served over a combination of 1/2 raw oysters and 1/2 cold, cooked shrimp (a great favorite in Mexico).

1 cup JELLED MILK, page 66
1 cup cold milk
2 teaspoons fructose
1/2 teaspoon vanilla (or
    any extract you like)

1 generous cup contains:
   Whole milk = 1 Whole Milk
      Exchange — 180 calories
   Low-fat = 1 Low-fat Milk
      Exchange — 135 calories
   Non-fat = 1 Non-fat Milk
      Exchange — 90 calories
   1/4 Fruit Exchange

2 cups WHIPPED MILK TOPPING,
   page 72
1 egg

1 generous cup contains:
   1 Whole Milk Exchange
   1/2 Medium-fat Meat Exchange
   1/4 Fruit Exchange
   218 calories

WHIPPED MILK TOPPING

Put all ingredients in the blender and blend on high speed until frothy. Cover and store in the refrigerator.

This topping is fabulous on fresh or poached fruit.

WHIPPED BUTTERMILK TOPPING

Use same procedure and ingredients as for WHIPPED MILK TOP-PING, but substitute WHIPPED BUTTERMILK for the WHIPPED MILK and cold buttermilk for the cold milk. I like to add more vanilla, too, perhaps a whole teaspoon. A generous cup contains 1 Non-fat Milk Exchange, 1/4 Fruit Exchange and 90 calories. I like this topping best with baked apples, pineapple and fresh oranges. It is also a good dressing on fruit salads.

INSTANT CUSTARD TOPPING

Dip raw egg in boiling water for 30 seconds and add to WHIPPED MILK TOPPING.

Variations: Add 1/4 teaspoon rum extract and sprinkle with nutmeg. Excellent served alone or with fruit.

STRAWBERRY JAM

Put the strawberries, whole, in a covered saucepan. Cook, covered, over very low heat without water for about 10 minutes. Remove the lid and bring the juice to the boiling point. Boil for 1 minute and remove from heat. Soften the gelatin in the lemon juice. Pour some of the hot juice from the strawberries into the gelatin. Stir until the gelatin is completely dissolved. Add the dissolved gelatin to the strawberries. Allow to cool to room temperature. Add fructose and refrigerate. Divine all by itself, but try it on French toast, plain old toast, English muffins, OR toast 1/2 a bagel, spread it with 1 tablespoon sour cream (only 1/2 Fat Exchange!) and top it all with this strawberry jam.

Variations: You can use this same recipe for any fresh fruit jam. However, I think it is best for peaches, pineapple and berries of all types.

3 cups fresh strawberries (or fresh frozen without sugar)
1-1/2 teaspoons lemon juice
1-1/2 teaspoons unflavored gelatin
2 teaspoons fructose

Makes 3 cups
1 cup contains:
1-1/2 Fruit Exchanges
60 calories

FRESH CRANBERRY RELISH

Wash oranges well and grate 2 tablespoons of orange peel. Be careful to grate only the orange-colored part of the peel. Peel oranges and cut them in pieces, removing seeds and connecting membranes. Put them in the blender with the fructose and grated peel. Mix well. Add the cranberries, a few at a time, until all of the berries have been blended into the relish. Don't blend it too fine, as you want a fairly coarse relish.

Make this several days before Thanksgiving, or whenever you plan to serve it. It is much better after sitting in the refrigerator for 3 or 4 days.

1 pound (4 cups) fresh cranberries
2 small oranges
2 tablespoons grated orange peel
2/3 cup fructose

Makes 4 cups
1/2 cup of relish contains:
1-1/2 Fruit Exchanges
60 calories

sauces/dressings

1 egg
1 cup low-fat milk
3/4 teaspoon fructose
1/4 teaspoon vanilla extract

Each recipe contains:
   1 Medium-fat Meat Exchange
   1 Low-fat Milk Exchange
   1/4 Fruit Exchange
   210 calories

1 cup plain low-fat yogurt
1/3 teaspoon fructose
1/2 teaspoon vanilla extract

1 cup contains:
   1 Low-fat Milk Exchange
   1/2 Fruit Exchange
   145 calories

EGG & MILK CEREAL TOPPING

Dip egg in boiling water for 30 seconds. Combine with other ingredients in the blender and blend until well mixed. Pour over cereal (1 Bread Exchange) and top this with chopped fruit (1 Fruit Exchange) and you have all your Exchanges for breakfast in one bowl!

SWEET YOGURT SAUCE

Add fructose and vanilla to yogurt, mix well.

salads

Salads, like soups , have great latitude in the Exchange Diet. They can be small dinner salads served as a side dish or a first course containing very little food value. Or you can make a large salad, containing all of the exchanges necessary for the meal, and serve it as the main course.

Salads can also be beautiful. Take the few extra minutes necessary to garnish your salads with radish roses, curled carrots, shredded parsley or mint, or something! Always serve salads very cold on chilled plates.

When using lettuce or other greens, wash them thoroughly a couple of hours before you plan to serve them. Pat them dry with paper towels and tear the greens into bite-sized pieces in a collander. Put the colander on top of another plate to drain and put it in the refrigerator until time to serve it. You will find that your salads will be more crisp and that it takes less salad dressing because the dressing is not diluted with unwanted water.

salads

1/2 head romaine lettuce, torn into
    bite-size pieces
1 bunch (1 handful) fresh spinach,
    torn in bite-size pieces
1 full recipe GARDEN SALAD
    DRESSING, page 64
1/2 head raw cauliflower, in small
    flowerettes
1 cucumber, very thinly sliced
2 zucchini squash, raw, thinly sliced
2 stalks celery, sliced
1 green pepper, without seeds,
    thinly sliced
6 radishes, thinly sliced
6 green onion tops, chopped
2 cups raw mushrooms, sliced
3 large, ripe tomatoes, diced
12 sprigs parsley for garnish

Makes 12 servings
Each serving contains:
    1-1/4 Fat Exchanges
    56 calories

GARDEN SALAD

Early in the day wash lettuce and spinach and tear it into bite-size pieces. Put it in the refrigerator. Make the GARDEN SALAD DRESSING and put it in the refrigerator. Just before serving prepare all of the other vegetables and toss them with the lettuce and spinach. Add the salad dressing and toss until all of the vegetables glisten. Serve on chilled plates and garnish with parsley sprigs.

Of course you can vary the proportions of this salad to suit your own taste and what is available. It is also good served with FRENCH DRESSING or ROQUEFORT DRESSING. The raw vegetables are all FREE FOODS so you only have to figure your dressing Exchanges.

CARROT SALAD

Mix all of the ingredients together well and serve on chilled plates.

3 cups carrots, peeled and grated
6 tablespoons raisins
6 tablespoons MAYONNAISE
   DRESSING, page 61

Makes 6 servings
Each serving contains:
   1 Vegetable Exchange
   1/2 Fruit Exchange
   1 Fat Exchange
   90 calories

salads

1 clove garlic, cut into quarters
1/2 cup salad oil or olive oil
2 heads romaine lettuce (12 cups cut
    in bite-size pieces)
1 raw egg
2 cups CROUTONS, page 143
    (4 slices bread)
1/2 cup Parmesan cheese, grated
2 teaspoons Worcestershire sauce
3/4 teaspoon salt
1/8 teaspoon black pepper, freshly
    ground
3 tablespoons lemon juice
9 flat filets of anchovies, chopped

Makes 8 servings
Each serving contains:
    3 Fat Exchanges
    1/2 Bread Exchange
    1/2 Low-fat Meat Exchange
    198 calories

CAESAR SALAD

The night before, or early in the morning, cut the garlic clove in quarters and drop it into a jar with a lid. Add the oil and cover. Allow to stand at room temperature until 1 hour before serving salad. Then put it in the refrigerator.

Several hours before serving, wash the romaine thoroughly and dry it. Tear into bite-size pieces and put in a large bowl lined with a cloth to absorb any remaining moisture. Store in the refrigerator.

Dip the raw egg in boiling water for 30 seconds. Then put it in the refrigerator to have cold when ready to use.

Just before serving, remove garlic from the oil. Put 2 tablespoons of the oil in a jar with the CROUTONS. Cover tightly and shake well. Add 2 tablespoons of the Parmesan cheese, and shake again.

Add the Worcestershire sauce, salt and pepper to the oil and shake.

Remove the cloth from under the lettuce and sprinkle the lettuce with the remaining Parmesan cheese and toss lightly. Drizzle oil over the salad and toss until every leaf glistens. Break the whole egg onto the salad, pour the lemon juice over it, and toss until the egg specks disappear. Add the CROUTONS, the chopped anchovies and toss lightly. Serve on large, chilled plates.

SPINACH SALAD

Early in the day wash the spinach, remove the center stem and tear the tender part of the leaf into bite-size pieces. Make the BACON DRESSING. Hard-boil the eggs. Store in the refrigerator all day.

Just before serving toss the spinach with the dressing until every leaf glistens. Shred the eggs. Serve the salad on chilled plates and top each serving with shredded egg.

Variation: Sprinkle 1/2 slice of crumbled bacon on the top of each serving along with the shredded egg. If you do this add 1/2 Fat Exchange to each serving.

1-1/2 pounds tender fresh spinach
(6 cups torn in bite-size pieces)
1/4 cup BACON DRESSING,
page 64
2 hard cooked eggs, shredded

Makes 8 servings
Each serving contains:
1 Fat Exchange
1/4 Medium-fat Meat Exchange
63 calories

COLD PEA SALAD IN THE BOWL . . . THREE DAYS OLD

Cook peas until almost done, then drain and cool. Mix together sour cream, green onion tops and seasoned salt. Fold into the cool green peas thoroughly. Chill in the refrigerator for 2 days before serving.

Variations: You can cut the Fat Exchanges in half by using 1/2 cup yogurt mixed with 1/2 cup sour cream instead of 1 cup of sour cream.

3 cups fresh, green peas
(or 2 packages frozen peas)
1 cup sour cream
1 cup green onion tops, chopped
finely
1 teaspoon seasoned salt

Makes 6 servings
(This will serve 12 if many other things are served.)
Each serving contains:
1 Vegetable Exchange
2-1/2 Fat Exchanges
138 calories

salads

1/2 teaspoon dry mustard
1/2 cup red wine vinegar
1/4 cup water
1/2 teaspoon oregano
1/2 teaspoon sweet basil
1/4 teaspoon freshly ground
   black pepper
3/4 teaspoon fructose
1 teaspoon salt
1/2 teaspoon Worcestershire sauce
2 cups young, green string beans,
   cooked
1/2 cup finely chopped onion

Makes 4 servings
Each serving contains:
   1 Vegetable Exchange
   25 calories

MARINATED GREEN BEAN SALAD

Mix the dry mustard with 1 tablespoon of the vinegar until completely dissolved. Add all of the other ingredients except beans and onion and mix well. Pour over cooked, drained green string beans and marinate for at least 2 hours before serving. Serve cold with finely chopped onion sprinkled over the top.

Variations: This is a good marinade for many other cold, cooked vegetables. Try it for brussels sprouts, asparagus, and zucchini, all excellent served with cold meat.

WILTED GERMAN SALAD

Put chopped tomatoes and onions in a bowl and add fructose and salt. Allow to stand at room temperature for about 3 hours. In a skillet put bacon fat, chopped bacon, and heat. Arrange shredded lettuce on 4 plates. Pour juice off tomatoes and onions into another bowl. Spoon tomatoes and onions on top of lettuce equally. Add vinegar to juice from tomatoes and onions and add juice to hot bacon fat. Bring sauce to a boil and pour equally over the 4 salads.

Variation: To cut the Fat Exchanges in half replace the 2 slices of BAKED BACON with 2 tablespoons of bacon bits (artificial).

3 tomatoes, peeled and finely chopped
1/2 cup finely chopped sweet onion
1-1/2 teaspoons fructose
1/2 teaspoon salt
2 slices BAKED BACON,
   chopped finely, page 126
2 teaspoons bacon fat
1 tablespoon cider vinegar
juice from tomatoes and onions
1 small head of lettuce, shredded

Makes 4 servings
Each serving contains:
   1 Vegetable Exchange
   1 Fat Exchange
   70 calories

salads

8 small stalks of celery, the tender
   ones close to the heart of the
   bunch, leaves included
2 cups CHICKEN BOUILLON,
   page 44, or enough to cover
   the celery in a saucepan
1 cup FRENCH DRESSING, page 62
   (double the recipe)
1/2 bud garlic, pressed
1/8 teaspoon celery seeds
2 tablespoons capers
2 tablespoons pimientos, chopped

Makes 4 servings
Each serving contains:
   1-1/2 Fat Exchanges
   1 Vegetable Exchange
   93 calories

CELERY VICTOR

Cook the celery stalks until they are tender, usually about 20 minutes, depending on the size celery. Drain the celery and lay it flat in a glass or plastic container. Add the garlic and celery seeds to the FRENCH DRESSING and pour this over the celery. Marinate all day or overnight before serving. To serve place 2 stalks on each plate and garnish with pimiento cut in thin strips and a few capers sprinkled on the top.

ANTIPASTO SALAD

Tear lettuce into bite-size pieces in a large salad bowl. Toss the lettuce thoroughly with the Parmesan cheese. Then toss the other ingredients into the salad, mixing completely. Add the ITALIAN DRESSING and mix well. Serve on very cold plates.

This is a fabulous first course for an Italian dinner! It is also a marvelous main course for a luncheon or light supper served with PIZZA MUFFINS. Or try it for a luncheon, serving PARTY PEARS in SAUTERNE SAUCE for dessert

1 large head red or Boston lettuce
    (about 6 cups bite-size pieces)
1/4 cup Parmesan cheese, grated
3/4 cup CAPONATA (cold eggplant
    appetizer), page 151
3/4 cup garbanzo beans
2 slices hard salami, chopped
1/2 cup (2 ounces) jack cheese, diced
2 filets of anchovy, drained and
    chopped (optional)
1/2 cup ITALIAN DRESSING,
    page 63

Makes 6 servings
Each serving contains:
    1 High-fat Meat Exchange
    1/4 Bread Exchange
    2 Fat Exchanges
    203 calories

salads

1 head cabbage, shredded (8 cups)
3/4 cup COLE SLAW DRESSING,
   page 66

Makes 12 servings
Each serving contains:
   1 Fat Exchange
   45 calories

3 cucumbers, peeled and sliced
   paper thin
1/2 teaspoon salt
1/4 cup white wine vinegar
1/4 cup water
1-1/2 teaspoons fructose
2 teaspoons dill weed

One recipe contains:
   1-1/2 Fruit Exchanges
   60 calories

COLE SLAW

Toss cabbage and dressing together well before serving.

Variations: Cole slaw is a marvelous base for many fruit and vegetable additions. Try it with: pineapple, grated carrots, apple, raisins, green bell pepper or cooked peas. Remember when adding fruit or vegetables to add the Exchanges and calories.

COLD CUCUMBERS IN DILL SAUCE

Place the sliced cucumbers in a shallow bowl and sprinkle them with salt. Cover the cucumbers and put them in the refrigerator for 2 hours. Pour the water off which has accumulated and add all the other ingredients, mixed together. Put the cucumbers back in the refrigerator for 2 hours before serving.

SUNRISE SALAD

At Romanoff's they used to call this Sunset Salad!

Shred cabbage and then wash it in a colander. Dry it thoroughly by putting it in a large dish towel. Hold the dish towel like a knapsack and shake it. Put the cabbage back in the colander. Put the colander on a plate in the refrigerator until ready to serve. (Cabbage, like lettuce and all other salad greens should be completely dry so that the dressing will adhere to it.)

Put all of the ingredients in a large, chilled salad bowl and toss well. Serve on 4 large chilled plates.

I love this salad served with thinly sliced toasted rye bread. You don't need butter on it; just toast it crisp.

6 cups raw cabbage, shredded
1/2 cup cold, cooked beef tongue, cut in thin strips
1/2 cup cold, cooked ham, cut in thin strips
1/2 cup cold, cooked chicken, cut in thin strips
1/2 cup Swiss cheese, cut in thin strips
1/2 cup FRENCH DRESSING, page 62

Makes 4 servings
Each serving contains:
    2 Medium-fat Meat Exchanges
    3 Fat Exchanges
    285 calories

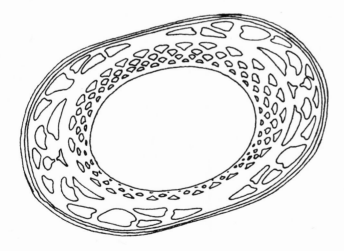

salads

10 walnut halves, cut in small pieces
1/2 teaspoon salt
1/4 cup shredded coconut
1 large head iceberg lettuce
   or 2 heads Boston lettuce
2/3 fresh papaya, finely diced
1/2 cup CURRY DRESSING, page 65

Makes 8 servings
Each serving contains:
   1-1/2 Fat Exchanges
   1/2 Fruit Exchange
   88 calories

CURRY-CONDIMENT SALAD

Salt and toast walnuts, page 181. Toast COCONUT, page 181. Cool before using. Wash and dry the lettuce. Tear into bite-size pieces (approximately 8 cups). In a large salad bowl, toss the lettuce, toasted walnuts and chopped fruit thoroughly with the CURRY DRESSING. Serve on very cold salad plates and sprinkle with toasted coconut. Try the CURRY-CONDIMENT SALAD as the first course with an Oriental dinner such as SWEET AND SOUR PORK or CHICKEN TERIYAKI.

Variations: If papaya is unavailable, 1 large apple or 1 cup of fresh chopped pineapple may be substituted. Just as the name of this salad suggests, any of the classic curry condiments may be used with great taste success! My favorite happens to be walnuts and papaya. So this is the way I give you the recipe. But for a complete and delicious change, try substituting 12 crushed peanuts for the walnuts and 1/4 cup raisins for the fruit.

TABBOULI
(Lebanese Salad)

Soak bulghar in hot water for 30 minutes. While the bulghar is soaking, make the dressing. Combine the lemon juice and salt and stir until the salt has dissolved. Add the pepper, garlic and water and mix well. Slowly add the oil. Put the dressing in a jar with a tightly fitted lid and shake vigorously for 30 seconds. Set aside.

Drain the bulghar thoroughly. Add the tomato, parsley, green onions and mint leaves to the bulghar. Add the dressing and toss thoroughly. Chill well.

Serve on chilled salad plates with each serving surrounded by 4 romaine leaves. Traditionally this salad is eaten by scooping it up on the romaine leaves.

1 cup uncooked bulghar
   (cracked wheat)
hot water to cover bulghar
1/4 cup lemon juice
1/2 teaspoon salt
1/4 teaspoon pepper, freshly ground
1 clove garlic, minced
1 tablespoon water
3 tablespoons olive oil
2 tomatoes, diced
4 green onions, chopped
1 cup parsley, minced
1/2 cup fresh mint leaves, minced
24 small romaine lettuce leaves

Makes 8 servings
Each serving contains:
   1 Bread Exchange
   1 Fat Exchange
   115 calories

87

salads

8 small heads Boston lettuce
2 cups (1 - #2 can) unsweetened
   pineapple chunks
4 cups cold roasted chicken cut
   into 1/2-inch cubes
20 broiled walnut halves, chopped
3/4 cup CURRY DRESSING,
   page 65
4 tablespoons TOASTED SHREDDED
   COCONUT , page 181

Makes 8 servings
Each serving contains:
  2 Low-fat Meat Exchanges
  2-1/4 Fat Exchanges
  3/4 Fruit Exchange
  241 calories

CHICKEN SALAD

Wash lettuce and remove hearts, being careful not to tear the outer leaves. Tear three of the hearts into bite-sized pieces (approximately 4 cups of torn lettuce). Retain the outer leaves for serving the salad. Drain pineapple chunks and cut each chunk in half. In a large mixing bowl toss together the lettuce, pineapple, chicken, walnuts and CURRY DRESSING until well mixed. Portion evenly onto 8 lettuce beds. Sprinkle with TOASTED SHREDDED COCONUT.

I like to serve this with a slice of chilled ripe papaya as a garnish, because it looks beautiful, tastes good, and brings the fruit up to 1 full exchange. I generally accompany my CHICKEN SALAD with slices of warm BANANA BREAD, page 142 and DESERT TEA, page 179. For dessert serve WHIPPED MILK TOPPING, page 72, with rum and vanilla flavoring.

SAVORY SEED SALAD

Toss all of the ingredients except the dressing together. When they are well mixed, dribble the dressing all over the salad. Toss until all of the vegetables glisten.

2 tablespoons TOASTED SESAME
SEEDS, page 181
3 tablespoons TOASTED
SUNFLOWER SEEDS, page 181
2 cups fresh alfalfa sprouts
2 cups fresh, raw mushrooms, sliced
3 cups butter lettuce, torn
into bite-size pieces
2 cups jack cheese, cut in very thin
strips
1/2 cup FRENCH DRESSING, page 62

Makes 8 servings
Each serving contains:
3 Fat Exchanges
1 High-fat Meat Exchange
230 calories

salads

1 envelope unflavored gelatin
1/4 cup cold water
3/4 cup hot CHICKEN STOCK, page 35
3/4 cup cold water

SOUFFLÉ TEXTURED ASPIC BASE

This is the basis for specific fish, chicken or meat aspics listed below. Add the gelatin (and lemon juice if used) to the 1/4 cup cold water to soften. Add the hot CHICKEN STOCK and dissolve completely. Put in the refrigerator and jell until firm. When firm, put into the blender with cold water and blend until frothy. Pour into a bowl and allow to stand a few minutes until the mixture starts to thicken. Fold in other ingredients called for in each recipe and pour into lightly oiled chilled salad mold (or 4 individual molds). Chill overnight before serving. Unmold carefully and serve on a bed of shredded lettuce. Garnish with cold marinated vegetables. Serve with dressing.

Serves 4
Each serving contains:
  2 Low-fat Meat Exchanges
  110 calories

SOUFFLÉ TEXTURED TUNA OR SALMON ASPIC

To aspic base, add 1-1/2 teaspoons lemon juice. Fold in 2 7-ounce cans white meat tuna or 2 cups salmon, 1/4 cup finely chopped green pepper and 1/4 cup finely chopped celery. Cut 2 hard-boiled eggs in round slices. Place egg slices and 1/3 cup pimiento strips in a design in the bottom of mold, before pouring in gelatin mixture. Serve with GREEN GODDESS DRESSING, page 62 or CREAMY TARRAGON DRESSING, page 68.

SOUFFLÉ TEXTURED HAM ASPIC

To aspic base, fold in 1 cup potatoes (cooked, cold and diced), 1-1/2 cups cooked diced ham, 3 tablespoons chopped onion and 2 teaspoons cider vinegar. Serve with MUSTARD SAUCE, page 58.

Makes 4 servings
Each serving contains:
  1-1/2 Low-fat Meat Exchanges
  1/4 Bread Exchange
  100 calories

SOUFFLÉ TEXTURED CHICKEN ASPIC #1

To basic recipe, add 1-1/2 cups chopped, cooked chicken; 1 stalk celery, finely chopped; 1/2 cup carrots, cooked and sliced thinly; 2 tablespoons minced parsley and 2 hard-boiled eggs, finely chopped. Serve with CREAMY TARRAGON DRESSING, page 68.

Makes 4 servings
Each serving contains:
  2 Low-fat Meat Exchanges
  1/4 Vegetable Exchange
  116 calories

SOUFFLÉ TEXTURED CHICKEN ASPIC #2

To basic recipe, add 2 cups chopped cooked chicken; 1 8-ounce can water chestnuts, thinly sliced; 1/2 cup pineapple chunks, drained (or 1/2 cup chopped fresh pineapple) and 1/4 cup sliced celery. Serve with shredded toasted coconut, chopped toasted walnuts and raisins. Top with CURRY DRESSING, page 65.

Makes 4 servings
Each serving contains:
  2 Low-fat Meat Exchanges
  1/4 Fruit Exchange
  120 calories

SOUFFLÉ TEXTURED BEEF ASPIC

Substitute 3/4 cup hot BEEF STOCK, for chicken stock in basic recipe. Then add 2 cups chopped, cooked beef and 1 cup MARINATED GREEN BEANS, page 80. Serve with HORSERADISH DRESSING, page 60.

Makes 4 servings
Each serving contains:
  2 Low-fat Meat Exchanges
  1/4 Vegetable Exchange
  116 calories

16 TOASTED TORTILLA
    TRIANGLES (4 corn tortillas
    toasted), page 143
1 cup pinto beans, cooked and
    mashed and warm, or refried beans
1/2 pound ground beef, without fat,
    cooked and crumbled and warm
1/4 cup Mexican salsa
    or taco sauce
6 cups shredded lettuce
1-1/2 cups cheddar cheese, grated
2 ripe tomatoes, diced
1 cup beets, cooked, cut in strips
    (optional)
1 cup carrots cut in strips
    (optional)
4 cups CREAMY TOSTADA
    TOPPING, page 69
4 tablespoons Parmesan cheese,
    grated

Makes 4 servings
Each serving contains:
    1 Bread Exchange
    3 Medium-fat Meat Exchanges
    1/2 Low-fat Milk Exchange
    1/4 Vegetable Exchange
    364 calories
    1-1/4 Vegetable Exchanges if you use
    beets and carrots

TOSTADAS

Use 4 large plates. On each plate arrange 4 TOASTED TORTILLA TRIANGLES. Spread the tortillas with the mashed beans, 1/4 cup per serving. Sprinkle the cooked ground meat, mixed with the Mexican salsa on top of the tortillas. Put equal amounts of the Mexican salsa or taco sauce on top of tortillas. Evenly sprinkle the tomato on top of the lettuce. If you are using beets and carrots put 1/4 cup of each one on the top of each tostada. Sprinkle the grated cheese evenly on the top of each tostada. Pour 1 cup of the CREAMY TOSTADA TOPPING on the top of each one and sprinkle 1 tablespoon of Parmesan cheese over it.

If you are allowed only 2 Meat Exchanges for the menu, use 2 tablespoons meat and 1/4 cup cheese.

Egg and cheese dishes offer great variety to the necessary Meat Exchanges. They can be served for breakfast, brunch, lunch or dinner with equal gourmet success.

egg and cheese dishes

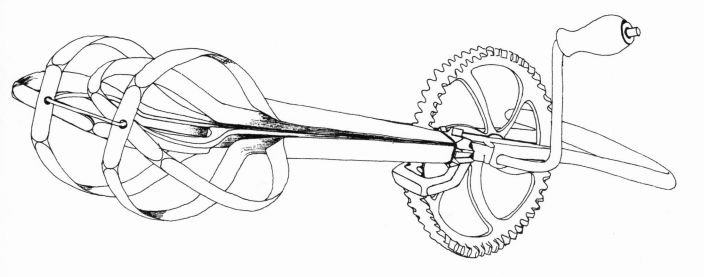

2 quarts water
2 tablespoons white vinegar
1 tablespoon lemon juice
1 teaspoon salt
eggs

Each egg contains:
1 Medium-fat Meat Exchange
75 calories

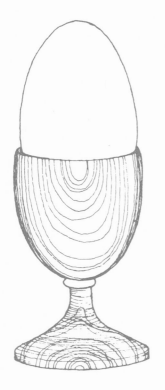

POACHED EGGS

Put the water, vinegar, lemon juice and salt in a large pan and bring to a boil. When the water is boiling, break each egg in a saucer, one at a time, and slide them into the water rapidly, so that they will cook evenly. Turn the heat down to simmer. Poach the eggs about 2 to 3 minutes, depending on how firm you want them. Do not put too many eggs in the pan at one time as they are difficult to handle.

Remove the eggs from the water with a slotted spoon. Dip each egg in a bowlful of warm water with a little salt in it to rinse the egg. Then blot it with a paper towel before serving.

Poached eggs may be made ahead and stored in the refrigerator. In order to store the eggs after poaching them, put them directly in a bowl full of ice water. I often make my poached eggs a day before I plan to serve them.

To serve the cold eggs, reheat them in a large pan of warm water with a little salt and bring it almost to a boil. Remove each egg and blot with a paper towel and serve it. No one will ever know when you originally cooked it.

EGGS BENEDICT

Toast the English muffins and spread each half with a little of the HAPPY HOLLANDAISE SAUCE.

Broil the Canadian bacon and cut each slice in 4 equal pieces. Put 3 of the pieces of Canadian bacon on each of the 4 muffin halves. Poach the eggs, leaving the yolk soft, and put 1 egg on each muffin. Spoon the remaining HAPPY HOLLANDAISE SAUCE equally on top of each egg. Place thinly sliced truffle on the top of each Egg Benedict for garnish.

2 English muffins, cut in halves
3 slices Canadian bacon
4 eggs, poached
3/4 cup HAPPY HOLLANDAISE
   SAUCE, page 60
2 truffles, thinly sliced (optional)

Makes 4 servings
Each serving contains:
   2 Medium-fat Meat Exchanges
   1-1/4 Bread Exchanges
   3/4 Fat Exchange
   271 calories

EGGS TOLSTOY

Spread each slice of pumpernickel bread with a little of the HAPPY HOLLANDAISE SAUCE.

Poach the eggs, leaving the yolk soft, and put an egg on top of each slice of bread. Mix the caviar with the remaining HAPPY HOLLANDAISE SAUCE and spoon it on top of each egg equally.

4 slices pumpernickel bread
4 eggs, poached
3/4 cup HAPPY HOLLANDAISE
   SAUCE, page 60
3 tablespoons caviar

Makes 4 servings
Each serving contains:
   2 Medium-fat Meat Exchanges
   1-1/4 Bread Exchanges
   3/4 Fat Exchange
   271 calories

eggs/cheese

1 tablespoon oil
1 onion, chopped
1 green bell pepper, chopped
   (without seeds)
2 buds garlic, pressed
1 28-ounce can (3-1/2 cups) peeled
   tomatoes, chopped with the juice
   from the can
3 green chilis, chopped with veins
   and seeds removed
1 teaspoon salt
1/3 teaspoon freshly ground black
   pepper
1 teaspoon chili powder
1 teaspoon oregano
1/2 teaspoon ground cumin
6 eggs, at room temperature
1-1/2 cups grated Monterey
   Jack Cheese
6 corn tortillas, hot

Makes 6 servings
Each serving contains:
   2 Medium-fat Meat Exchanges
   1 Bread Exchange
   1/2 Fat Exchange
   1 Vegetable Exchange
   268 calories

HUEVOS RANCHEROS
(Ranch Style Eggs)

In a **cured** heavy iron skillet, heat the oil. Add the onion, green bell pepper and garlic. Cook until the onion is clear. Add all of the other ingredients except the eggs, cheese and tortillas and cook for 20 minutes.

Carefully place the eggs on top of the sauce, making a little depression for each egg. Sprinkle the grated cheese all over the top. Cover and cook for 10 to 12 minutes or until the egg whites are white and the cheese is melted.

Serve each egg on top of a hot tortilla. Spoon the remaining sauce over the top of each serving.

FRENCH TOAST

Beat the egg in a shallow bowl with a fork. Put the slice of bread in the bowl, turning it over occasionally until all of the egg is absorbed. Cook it in a Teflon skillet or cured heavy iron skillet until lightly browned on both sides.

1 egg
1 slice bread

Each serving contains:
   1 Bread Exchange
   1 Medium-fat Meat Exchange
   145 calories

BUTTERMILK FRENCH TOAST

Beat the eggs with a fork in a shallow dish. Add the buttermilk and salt and mix well. Dip each slice of bread in the mixture turning it over to soak up the liquid.

If butter is used for cooking, remember 1 teaspoon of butter equals 1 Fat Exchange. French toast is good served with STRAWBERRY JAM. Also, try serving it with CITRUS SAUCE.

3 eggs
1/2 cup buttermilk
1/8 teaspoon salt
6 slices bread
OR
1 egg
4 teaspoons buttermilk
1 slice bread

Makes 6 servings
Each serving contains:
   1 Bread Exchange
   1/2 Medium-fat Meat Exchange
   108 calories

12 eggs, hard-boiled
2 cups MORNAY SAUCE, page 57
1 tablespoon prepared mustard
1/2 teaspoon Worcestershire sauce
1/4 cup Romano cheese, grated

Makes 12 servings
Each serving contains:
   2-1/4 Medium-fat Meat Exchanges
   1/4 Fat Exchange
   1/4 Whole Milk Exchange
   221 calories

HOT DEVILED EGGS

Cut the eggs in half lengthwise. Remove yolks and rub them through a sieve. Arrange the egg whites in a shallow glass baking dish. Add the mustard, Worcestershire sauce and sieved egg yolks to 1/2 cup of the MORNAY SAUCE. Mix well and fill the 24 egg white halves equally with the mixture.

Pour the remaining 1-1/2 cups of MORNAY SAUCE over the tops of the eggs. Sprinkle evenly with the Romano cheese. Bake at 425° for 15 minutes, or until the eggs are lightly browned.

This is a marvelous brunch dish. I like to serve it with CITRUS SAUCE COMPOTE and BANANA BREAD.

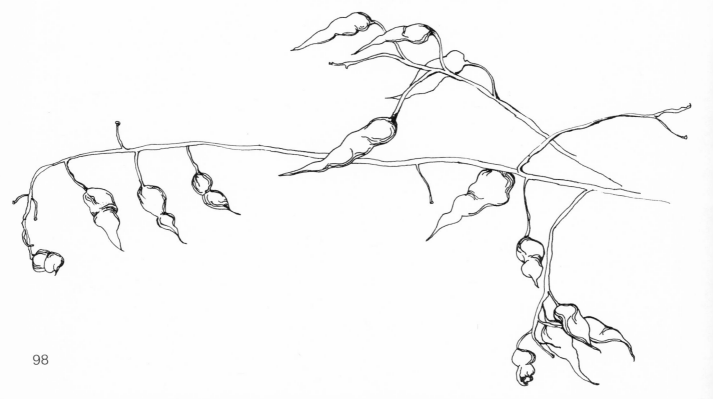

CHEESE SOUFFLÉ

Preheat oven to 400°. Put milk in a saucepan on low heat. Put butter in another, large saucepan. Melt butter and add flour, stirring constantly. Cook the flour and butter for 3 minutes. Do not brown. Take the flour-butter mixture off the heat and pour in the boiling milk, all at once, stirring with a wire whisk. Put the pan back on the heat and allow to come to a boil, stirring constantly. Boil for 1 minute. At this point the sauce will be quite thick. Remove from heat. Add the 4 egg yolks 1 at a time, stirring each one in thoroughly with a wire whisk. Add the salt, white pepper and Worcestershire sauce. **Stop!**

You can make this much of a soufflé ahead of time if you are entertaining. Cover the saucepan, re-heat the mixture to lukewarm before adding the beaten egg whites. Or you can go right ahead and finish the soufflé; it will be ready 20 to 25 minutes later! Add the cheese to the sauce and stir well. Put the egg whites in a large mixing bowl. Add a pinch of salt and the cream of tartar. Beat whites until stiff. Add 1/4 of the egg whites to the cheese sauce and stir them in. Add the remaining 3/4 egg whites to the cheese sauce and very carefully fold them in, being sure not to over-mix! Pour the mixture into an 8-inch soufflé dish. Place it in the center of the oven, preheated to 400°. Immediately turn the oven down to 375°. Cook the soufflé 20 to 25 minutes and serve immediately.

Variations: Add 1 tablespoon minced onion to the butter and cook slightly before adding the flour. Add 1 tablespoon imitation bacon bits at the same time as you add the cheese. Or try both the onion and the imitation bacon bits in the same soufflé.

1 cup milk
4 teaspoons butter
2-1/2 tablespoons flour
4 egg yolks
1/2 teaspoon salt
1/8 teaspoon white pepper
1/4 teaspoon Worcestershire sauce
1/2 cup grated cheese, Swiss, cheddar,
    Monterey Jack, Romano,
    Parmesan or a combination!
5 egg whites, at room temperature
pinch of salt
1/8 teaspoon cream of tartar

Makes 4 servings
Each serving contains:
    1-1/2 Medium-fat Meat Exchanges
    1 Fat Exchange
    1/4 Bread Exchange
    1/4 Whole Milk Exchange
    219 calories

8 CRÊPES, page 145
2 cups cottage cheese
1-1/2 tablespoons grated orange peel
3 tablespoons orange juice
1/2 teaspoon vanilla
1/8 teaspoon salt
1-1/2 tablespoons fructose

Makes 8 servings
Each serving contains:
    1/2 Bread Exchange
    1-1/4 Medium-fat Meat Exchanges
    129 calories

4 slices dry white bread
1 cup grated cheddar cheese
    (1/4 pound)
1/4 teaspoon Beau Monde seasoning
1/8 teaspoon white pepper
1/4 teaspoon dry mustard
1/4 teaspoon salt
4 eggs, lightly beaten
2 cups whole milk
2 tablespoons minced chives
    or green onion tops
1/4 teaspoon Worcestershire sauce

Makes 4 servings
Each serving contains:
    1 Bread Exchange
    2 Medium-fat Meat Exchanges
    1/2 Whole Milk Exchange
    305 calories

CHEESE BLINTZES

Warm the crepes so that they are pliable. Put the cottage cheese in a sieve and press out any liquid with the back of a spoon. Then put the drained cottage cheese in a bowl with all the other ingredients and mix well. Spoon the cottage cheese mixture evenly down the center of each crepe. Roll the crepe around the cheese and place it fold side down in a flat Teflon baking dish.

Bake at 425° for 10 minutes or until the tops are lightly browned. This much can be done in advance (even a day before). Cover the dish tightly and store in the refrigerator. To serve, bring it to room temperature first and then reheat in the oven.

These crepes are marvelous for a Christmas brunch, served with sliced cold turkey, FRESH CRANBERRY RELISH and BANANA BREAD!

FONDUE SOUFFLÉ

Allow bread to stand out on a counter exposed to the air for several hours, so that it can be easily cubed. Cut the bread in 1/4-inch squares. Arrange 1/2 of the bread cubes in a flat baking dish. Sprinkle 1/2 of the cheese evenly over the top of the bread, repeat, putting the remaining cheese on top. Stir all the seasonings into the eggs. Add milk; then green onion tops and the Worcestershire sauce. Pour the liquid mixture over the cheese and bread in the baking dish. Cover and refrigerate overnight. Remove from the refrigerator 2 hours before cooking. To cook, set the baking dish in a shallow pan of cold water and place it in a cold oven. Set the oven for 300° and cook for 1 hour. Check to make sure it is not getting too brown.

EGGS FOO YUNG

Put the soy sauce, cornstarch, vinegar and salt in a saucepan and stir until smooth. Slowly stir in the water. Cook over low heat, stirring constantly, until thickened. Add the fructose and set aside to spoon over the Egg Foo Yung patties.

To make the patties, put the bean sprouts, onions and shrimp in a bowl and mix together. Beat eggs lightly, add to this mixture and mix well with the other ingredients.

Put the oil in a cured heavy iron skillet and heat. When the skillet is hot, pour the egg mixture like pancakes, using about 1/4 cup per patty.

When lightly browned on one side, turn over and brown the other side. Then turn the heat low and continue cooking until the egg is completely done, about 5 minutes. Serve with a little of the sauce spooned over each Egg Foo Yung patty.

SAUCE
2 tablespoons soy sauce
2 teaspoons cornstarch
1 tablespoon cider vinegar
1/4 teaspoon salt
1/2 cup cold water
3/4 teaspoon fructose

EGGS FOO YUNG
1 cup bean sprouts,
    cooked and drained
1/2 cup minced green onion tops
1 cup shrimp, cooked and chopped
6 eggs
2 teaspoons cooking oil

Makes 4 servings
Each serving contains:
    2 Medium-fat Meat Exchanges
    1/4 Bread Exchange
    1/2 Fat Exchange
    191 calories

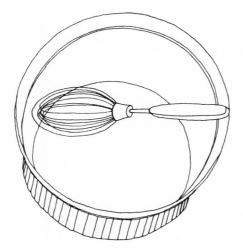

2 eggs
dash salt
dash pepper
1/2 teaspoon butter
1 tablespoon water

Makes 1 serving
1 omelette contains:
  2 Medium-fat Meat Exchanges
  1/2 Fat Exchange
  173 calories

OMELETTES

Beat eggs with a fork until frothy. Add 1 tablespoon water, salt and pepper and beat again. Meanwhile, melt butter in omelette pan (or 10-inch cured iron skillet with slanted sides) 'til sizzling hot. Turn flame down and pour in beaten egg. The egg immediately starts to "set." Using a fork, scrape the set edges of the egg towards the center, tilting the pan at the same time, so that the liquid egg then seeps underneath to cook. When bottom is cooked, (the top still runny), fold over 1/3 of the omelette towards the center. Rest the edge of the pan on the plate and quickly turn the pan upside down, so omelette slides out on plate, folded in thirds.

Variations: You may make many different types of omelettes. Have whatever you are going to put in the omelette ready when you put the eggs in the pan. Then before folding the omelette, put the other ingredients on top of the eggs and fold them into the center. Try filling omelettes with seafood, vegetables, fruit or create a new variety with bits of leftovers.

CHEESE OMELETTE
Add 1/4 cup grated cheese. Add to basic recipe: 1 High-fat Meat Exchange and 95 calories.

CHILI AND CHEESE OMELETTE
Add 1 can chopped Ortega chilis and 1/4 cup grated cheese. Add to basic recipe: 1 High-fat Meat Exchange and 95 calories.

JAM OR JELLY OMELETTE
Add 1/3 cup STRAWBERRY JAM, page 73. Add to basic recipe: 3/4 Fruit Exchange and 30 calories.

HAM OMELETTE

Add 1/4 cup cooked ham, chopped, 2 tablespoons green bell pepper, chopped, and 1 teaspoon onion, chopped. Add to basic recipe: 1 Low-fat Meat Exchange and 55 calories.

MEXICAN OMELETTE

Add 1/2 cup sauce from CHILI RELLENO recipe, page 132. No added calories.

CREOLE OMELETTE

Add 1/2 cup CREOLE GUMBO, page 111. Add to basic recipe: 1/2 Low-fat Meat Exchange, 1/4 Vegetable Exchange and 34 calories.

PIZZA MUFFINS

2 English muffins
1/4 cup TOMATO JUICE CATSUP, page 70
1/4 teaspoon oregano
1 cup grated mozzarella or Monterey Jack cheese (1/4 pound)
freshly ground black pepper

Makes 4 servings
Each serving contains:
1 Bread Exchange
1 High-fat Meat Exchange
165 calories

Cut English muffins in half and roll with rolling pin until each half is flat and larger in diameter. Spread each half with the tomato sauce mixed with the oregano. Sprinkle 1/4 of the grated cheese on top. Place the muffins on a cookie sheet and bake in a 425° oven for 8 to 10 minutes or until the cheese is bubbling and starting to brown.

To freeze: Put the pizzas on a cookie sheet; place under the broiler until the cheese just starts to melt. Cool, and place pizza muffins in individual plastic bags. Store in the freezer. When ready to serve, cook the same way as if unfrozen. It just takes a couple of minutes longer.

Variations: On top of the cheese you may want to add something else, such as: sliced mushrooms, chopped green pepper, chopped onion, anchovies, chopped bacon or imitation bacon bits, sardines, clams, crumbled ground beef or chopped ham.

These Pizza Muffins, served with a salad, make a great lunch or dinner. They also make fabulous hors d'oeuvre for other people!

fish and seafood

Fish and seafood are ideal for gourmet cooking in a low-fat diet because they contain so little saturated fats compared to beef, lamb, pork and ham.

Also, the delicate flavor of most fish lends itself well to a variety of seasonings.

I like to cook more fish than I need for one meal and use the cold leftovers chopped up in a fish salad. Try it! It's delicious and the fish is so low in fat that one extra teaspoon of salad dressing can be squeezed in on the sly!

POACHED SALMON
(Hot or Cold)

Bring COURT BOUILLON to a slow boil. Wrap the cheesecloth around the salmon so that it can be lifted out of the liquid easily in one piece when it is done. Place the salmon in the simmering bouillon for about 30 minutes.

To serve hot, lift the salmon out of the liquid. Carefully remove it from the cheesecloth and place it on a serving platter.

I like to serve hot poached salmon with HAPPY HOLLANDAISE SAUCE, page 60, mixed with capers and hot ONION-DILL BREAD. Add a colorful selection of your favorite vegetables steamed "just done" and arrange them on the platter around the salmon.

To serve cold: Lift the salmon out of the liquid and place it on a rack where it can drain (2 cake-cooling racks placed together work beautifully). Carefully remove the cheesecloth and peel the salmon. Allow the salmon to cool and cover it with MILK GLAZE, page 55. Allow the glaze to cool slightly and pour it over the salmon. You may need to put on 2 coats of the glaze. Allow the glaze to set until firm. Decorate with raw vegetables cut in fancy shapes.

Serve with MAYONNAISE DRESSING,   page 61, with capers added. I like hot ONION-DILL BREAD with cold salmon, too!

COURT BOUILLON, page 38
salmon, whole, or amount of
    steaks desired
piece of cheesecloth large enough
    to wrap salmon

1 ounce (1/4 cup) salmon contains:
    1 Low-fat Meat Exchange
    55 calories

fish

1-1/2 pounds red snapper
2 limes
1 teaspoon salt
2 teaspoons oil
1 cup sliced onion
1 4-1/2-ounce can pimientos
3 large ripe tomatoes, chopped
1 small green chili (or 1 teaspoon
   canned green chili, chopped)
10 capers, chopped
1 sprig parsley

Makes 8 servings
Each serving contains:
   2 Low-fat Meat Exchanges
   1/4 Fat Exchange
   1/4 Vegetable Exchange
   127 calories

RED SNAPPER VERACRUZ STYLE

Wash fish thoroughly with cold water. Squeeze lime juice on the fish, and rub with salt. Put in the refrigerator until ready to cook (at least 2 hours).

Put the oil in a cured, heavy iron skillet and heat. Add onion and cook until tender. Chop half of the pimientos and reserve the other half for garnish. Add chopped pimiento, tomatoes, chili and capers plus the sprig of whole parsley to the onions. Cook, covered, until there is about 1 inch of juice in the skillet. Add the fish and cook about 6 minutes on each side, or until the fish is completely white and fork-tender. Serve with the sauce spooned over the top. Remove parsley. Garnish with remaining pimiento.

STUFFED FILET OF SOLE

In the morning: Melt the butter and cook the mushrooms, onions and parsley until the onion is tender. Sprinkle both sides of each sole filet with salt, white pepper and paprika. Spoon the mushroom-onion-parsley mixture equally onto each filet. Fold over end of each filet to form a little roll and fasten with a toothpick. Place the stuffed filets in a baking dish, 12x8x2 inches.

Combine the BASIC WHITE SAUCE and sherry, mixing well, and spoon it over the stuffed filets. Sprinkle the top with grated cheese. Put the baking dish, covered, in the refrigerator until 1 hour before you plan to cook it.

One hour before cooking: Remove stuffed filets from refrigerator. Preheat oven to 400°. Sprinkle the top of the dish with a little paprika for added color. Bake for 30 minutes.

4 teaspoons butter
2 cups fresh mushrooms, thinly sliced
1/2 cup minced onion
1 tablespoon minced parsley
8 sole filets
salt
white pepper
paprika
2 cups BASIC WHITE SAUCE,
    page 55
1/3 cup sherry
1/2 cup grated cheddar cheese

Makes 8 servings
Each serving contains:
    2 Low-fat Meat Exchanges
    1 Fat Exchange
    1/4 Whole Milk Exchange
    187 calories

1-1/2 cups BASIC WHITE SAUCE,
    page 55
6 tablespoons HAPPY HOLLANDAISE
    SAUCE, page 60
8 CREPES, page 145
1 tablespoon butter
1 teaspoon minced shallots
1-1/2 cups crab meat
1/2 cup dry white wine
1 teaspoon curry powder
1/4 teaspoon Worcestershire sauce
1/4 teaspoon salt
1/8 teaspoon freshly ground
    black pepper

Makes 8 servings
Each serving contains:
    1 Fat Exchange
    3/4 Bread Exchange
    1 Low-fat Meat Exchange
    1/4 Whole Milk Exchange
    196 calories

CURRIED CRAB CREPES

Make the WHITE SAUCE, HAPPY HOLLANDAISE SAUCE, and CREPES.

Melt the butter in a cured, heavy iron skillet and sauté the shallots and crab meat together for 5 minutes. Add the wine, curry powder, Worcestershire sauce, salt and pepper and cook, stirring about 3 minutes. Remove from the heat and add 1 cup of the BASIC WHITE SAUCE. Mix well. Fill each crepe with 1/8 of the curried crab mixture and place it in a flat baking dish.

Mix the remaining 1/2 cup of BASIC WHITE SAUCE with the HAPPY HOLLANDAISE SAUCE and top each crepe with the sauce. Put the crepes under the broiler until they are a golden brown.

You can make the crepes ahead and store them, covered, in the refrigerator. Before serving, put them in a 350° oven for 10 minutes, then under the broiler until brown!

CALCUTTA CURRY

In a large pot melt butter. Add the minced onion and cook until the onion is clear and tender. Combine the flour, curry powder, salt and ground ginger. Add the flour mixture to the onions, stirring constantly, until it becomes a thick paste. Add the chicken stock and stir until it again becomes a thick paste. Slowly add the warm milk, stirring constantly. Cook slowly, stirring regularly, until the sauce has thickened (about 45 minutes). It never gets very thick! Add the shrimp and lemon juice. Heat thoroughly and serve over plain white rice.

Make a large selection of condiments, including many FREE FOODS allowed in any quantity! Major Grey's Chutney for Other People, Indian Chutney, raisins, chopped peanuts, bacon bits, shredded coconut, chopped hard-boiled egg, diced tomatoes, minced parsley, chopped pickles, grated orange peel and grated lemon peel.

3 tablespoons butter
3 onions, minced
5 tablespoons flour
1 tablespoon curry powder
1 teaspoon salt
1/4 teaspoon ground ginger
1 cup chicken stock
3 cups milk, warmed
2 pounds (6 cups) shrimp, cooked and
    cleaned or
    1/2 pound chicken (6 cups)
1 teaspoon lemon juice

Makes 8 servings
Each serving contains:
    2-1/4 Low-fat Meat Exchanges
    1 Fat Exchange
    1 Vegetable Exchange
    1/4 Bread Exchange
    210 calories
Cooked white rice (1/2 cup) contains:
    1 Bread Exchange
    70 calories

fish

2 cups (16-ounce can) cooked salmon
2 lightly beaten eggs
1 cup low-fat milk
2 tablespoons finely chopped
   green pepper
1 tablespoon finely chopped onion
2 tablespoons lemon juice
1/2 teaspoon salt
1/8 teaspoon white pepper
1/4 teaspoon Worcestershire sauce

Makes 4 servings
Each serving contains:
   2-1/2 Low-fat Meat Exchanges
   1/4 Low-fat Milk Exchange
   170 calories

SALMON LOAF

Mix all the ingredients together and pour into a loaf pan. Bake at 350° for 35 minutes, or until firm.

Serve hot with a green salad or serve cold with a hot vegetable. Also try it cold as a sandwich spread.

Variations: Use tuna instead of salmon.

CREOLE GUMBO

In a hot, cured, heavy iron skillet, put 1/4 cup juice from the tomatoes. Add the onions, garlic, green pepper, parsley and sauté until the onions are tender and clear. Chop the canned tomatoes and put them in a large kettle with the remaining tomatoes. Simmer for 1 hour. Do not wash pan. Add water and all seasonings and simmer for 1 hour. In cured skillet, fry okra until tender. Add the okra to the kettle. Add the tomato sauce and cook for 1/2 hour. Add crab and shrimp and cook for 30 more minutes.

I like to make the sauce the day before I am going to serve it to let all the flavors blend. Reheat it and add the seafood just before serving. Serve over cooked white rice.

2 28-ounce cans solid-pack tomatoes
   (plus the juice from the cans)
1 large onion, chopped
3 buds garlic, minced
1 green bell pepper, diced
3 sprigs parsley, chopped
4 cups water
1 teaspoon salt
1 teaspoon freshly ground
   black pepper
2 bay leaves
4 cups okra, cut in pieces
2 8-ounce cans tomato sauce
3/4 pound crab meat
3/4 pound raw shrimp
   (peeled and veined)

Makes 8 servings
Each serving contains:
   2 Low-fat Meat Exchanges
   2 Vegetable Exchanges
   160 calories
1/2 cup rice contains:
   1 Bread Exchange
   70 calories

fish

4 teaspoons oil
1 large onion, chopped
8 whole green onions, tops included
1 green bell pepper, seeded
   and chopped
2 buds garlic, whole
1/2 cup minced parsley
1 16-ounce can tomato purée
1 8-ounce can tomato sauce
1 cup water
1 cup dry white wine
1 bay leaf
1/8 teaspoon rosemary
1/8 teaspoon thyme
2 teaspoons salt
1/4 teaspoon freshly ground
   black pepper
2 medium crabs, cracked
16 clams in the shells
1 pound large shrimp or
   prawns in the shells

Makes 8 servings
Each serving contains:
   3-1/2 Low-fat Meat Exchanges
   1/2 Fat Exchange
   1 Vegetable Exchange
   241 calories

CIOPPINO

Heat oil in a large pot or soup kettle. Cook onion, green onions, green bell pepper and garlic until onion is clear but not browned, about 5 minutes. Add parsley, tomato purée, tomato sauce, water, wine and all seasonings. Cover and simmer for 1 hour.

Break the crab into pieces. Scrub the clams with a brush, making sure all sand is removed. Cut the shrimp down the back with scissors, wash and remove veins.

Remove the garlic from the pot. Add the crab first, then the clams and shrimp. Cook, covered, until the clams are open and the shrimp turns pink, about 20 minutes.

Serve with a tossed green salad with ITALIAN DRESSING and crusty San Francisco sour dough French bread. I always have bibs for my guests when I serve CIOPPINO. It is delicious, fun to eat, but messy!

GEFILTE FISH

Cut fish in cubes. Add onion, celery, garlic, marjoram, salt and pepper. Put all ingredients through a food grinder twice. Put ground ingredients in a large bowl and add beaten eggs, parsley, matzo meal, and mix well. Add milk slowly until all of the milk is absorbed. Mold fish into oblong pieces (about 20) and arrange in a large Teflon pan. Add thinly sliced carrots. On each fish cake place a small slice of lemon. Add FISH STOCK and simmer for 1/2 hour on very low heat. Remove from heat and cool. When cooled put in the refrigerator until thoroughly chilled and slightly jellied.

1-1/2 pounds white fish
1 pound sea bass
1 medium-size onion, chopped
1/2 cup chopped celery
3 buds garlic, minced
1/4 teaspoon marjoram
1/4 teaspoon salt
1/4 teaspoon salt
1/4 teaspoon white pepper
2 eggs, well beaten
1/4 cup finely chopped parsley
1-1/2 cups matzo meal or white
   bread crumbs
1-1/2 cups milk
2 carrots, sliced
3 lemons, peeled and sliced
8 cups FISH STOCK, page 38

Makes 16 servings
Each serving contains:
   1/2 Bread Exchange
   1-1/4 Low-fat Meat Exchanges
   104 calories

fish

1 16-ounce jar fresh oysters
1 pound fresh spinach, chopped
2 cups (1 recipe) MORNAY SAUCE,
    page 57
1 tablespoon Parmesan cheese
paprika

Makes 4 servings
Each serving contains:
    1-1/2 Low-fat Meat Exchanges
    3/4 Fat Exchange
    1/2 Whole Milk Exchange
    1/4 Bread Exchange
    217 calories

4 tablespoons soft butter or corn
    oil margarine (1/2 cube)
2 teaspoons minced garlic
1 teaspoon minced shallots
2 tablespoons minced parsley
24 snails
24 snail shells

Makes 4 servings
Each serving contains:
    3 Fat Exchanges
    3/4 Medium-fat Meat Exchange
    189 calories

OYSTERS FLORENTINE

Preheat oven to 350°. Cook the spinach and drain thoroughly. Heat the skillet and add oysters with 2 tablespoons of their own liquid. Cook until the edges curl and the oysters turn white, about 5 minutes. Line the bottom of a 12x8-inch glass baking dish with the spinach. Place the oysters on top of the spinach and pour the pan juices over the top. Cover with MORNAY SAUCE. Sprinkle with Parmesan cheese and a little paprika. Bake for 10 minutes and then lightly brown under the broiler.

Try serving this with CONSOMMÉ MADRILÈNE to start, TOASTED PILAF and BUTTERMILK BAKED TOMATOES. For dessert, fresh pineapple with INSTANT CUSTARD SAUCE. I like to sprinkle a little toasted coconut on top of the custard sauce when serving it with pineapple!

LES ESCARGOTS MAISON

Combine the butter, garlic, shallots and parsley. Cover and leave at room temperature until 1 hour before serving. Then put a little of the butter mixture into each snail shell. Put the snails in the shell, leaving the little curved part outside of the shells. Put the remaining butter on top of the snails in the shells.

Just before serving, preheat the oven to 550°. Put the snails in escargot dishes. Place the dishes in the oven for about 7 minutes, or until the butter is slightly browned.

Serve LES ESCARGOTS MAISON with lots of crusty French bread.

Of course, you can easily cut this to fewer Fat Exchanges by using less butter.

CEVICHE

Place cubed fish in a glass dish and pour lime juice over it. Lightly sprinkle salt, pepper and garlic salt over the raw fish. Cover and put in the refrigerator for 24 hours. Then add the remaining ingredients. Refrigerate 4 more hours before serving.

1 pound red snapper, cut
   in small cubes
juice of 3 limes
salt
pepper
garlic salt
1 cup chopped onion
1/4 cup red wine vinegar
2 teaspoons oregano
1/2 cup chopped fresh cilantro
   or parsley
3 ripe tomatoes, peeled and chopped
1 4-ounce can jalapeno chilis, cut in
   strips with the juice from the can
1 2-ounce can pimientos, in strips with
   the juice from the can
4 fresh small green chilis,
   chopped (optional)
1/2 cup TOMATO JUICE CATSUP,
   page 70
salt and freshly ground black
   pepper to taste

Makes 8 servings (as an appetizer)
Each serving contains:
   2 Low-fat Meat Exchanges
   1 Vegetable Exchange
   135 calories

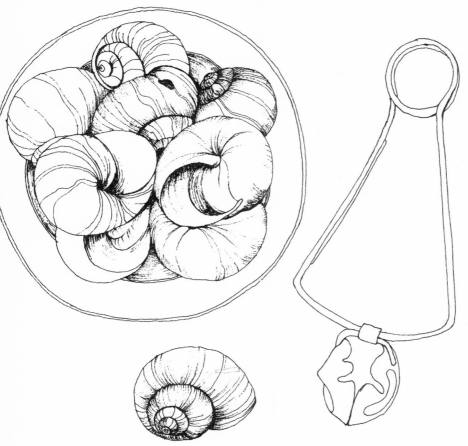

fish

2 teaspoons butter or corn oil
   margarine
2 8-ounce cans chopped clams,
   including juice
2 buds garlic, pressed
1 large eggplant, peeled and cut
   into 1/2-inch cubes
1/4 cup minced fresh parsley
1/4 cup minced fresh chives
   (or green onion tops)
1/4 cup grated Parmesan cheese
1/4 cup more minced fresh parsley!

Makes 4 servings
Each serving contains:
   1 Low-fat Meat Exchange
   1 Vegetable Exchange
   1/2 Fat Exchange
   103 calories

EGGPLANT NEPTUNE
(Eggplant in Clam Sauce)

In a cured, heavy iron skillet put butter and the liquid from the cans of chopped clams. Add the pressed garlic and cook slowly. Put the cubed eggplant into the clam juice and cook, stirring from time to time, for about 15 minutes. Add the first 1/4 cup minced parsley and the minced chives and cook for 5 minutes more. Add the chopped clams, grated Parmesan cheese and the remaining 1/4 cup of fresh parsley. Mix well and serve at once. Further cooking will make the clams tough!

meat and poultry

It is best to get in the habit of serving meat and poultry in a very straightforward manner—either broiled, roasted or boiled. It is easier to quickly judge exact portions allowed on your diet program and to reduce the amount of fat remaining in the meat.

When broiling or roasting, always put the meat on a rack with slots or holes in it. This allows the fat to drain properly from the meat.

When boiling or poaching, always refrigerate the meat in its liquid until the fat solidifies on the top so that it can be removed completely

There are times, however, when it is fun to take a more gourmet approach in preparing meat and poultry. On these occasions you will find the recipes in this book add great variety to your menus.

1 6-pound roast
1 bud garlic
salt

Each slice (3 x 2 x 1/8 inches)
contains:
    1 Low-fat Meat Exchange
    55 calories

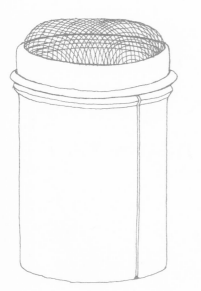

RAPID ROAST

My favorite roasts are prime rib of beef and leg of lamb. Preheat the oven to 500°. Rub the roast with garlic and salt it generously. Put the roast in the oven for 30 minutes and turn the heat *off.* Do not open the oven door for exactly 2 hours, then open it and remove the roast. Allow the roast to stand 15 minutes before carving as you will find it is much easier to slice.

To serve the roast au jus, use BEEF STOCK, page 34, or DE-FATTED DRIPPINGS, page 52, from your freezer. Because so little of the juice is lost in this method of cooking, you will find the drippings are almost 100 percent fat.

30 minutes will make a rare roast. If you wish a more well-done meat, then cook it for 33 or 34 minutes at 500° before turning the heat off. The general rule is: 5 minutes to the pound for rare and 5-1/2 to 6 minutes to the pound for more well-done meat.

If you wish to serve YORKSHIRE PUDDING, page 147, with your roast beef, use DEFATTED DRIPPINGS or BEEF STOCK from your freezer and, hopefully, another oven!

STEAK AU POIVRE
(Black Pepper Steak!)

Prepare the steak 2 hours before serving. Remove all fat, wipe the steak with a damp cloth and carefully dry it. Crush the peppercorns in a mortar with a pestle or put them in a cloth and pound them with a hammer! This amount makes a very hot pepper steak. If you prefer a mild flavor, use only 1 or 2 teaspoons of crushed peppercorns. Press the crushed peppercorns firmly into both sides of the steak. After pressing them in by hand I smack the steak all over with the flat side of a meat cleaver to press the pepper in more securely. Cover the steak and allow it to stand at room temperature until you are ready to cook it.

In a large cured iron skillet melt the butter. When butter is melted, wipe it out with a paper towel. Get the skillet very hot, put the steak in it and cook over very high heat for 5 minutes on each side (for rare steak).

Remove the steak to a heated platter. Into the hot skillet pour white wine and brandy. Allow to boil for 2 minutes, stirring constantly and scraping all the drippings at the bottom of the pan into the wine.

Remove the wine from the heat and the optional tablespoon butter (or less if you can't spare the Fat Exchanges) to the wine. Stir well and pour into a heated sauce dish or gravy boat. Slice the steak horizontally in very thin slices. Spoon a little of the sauce over each serving. I always cook a 3-pound steak no matter how many people I am serving, because it makes marvelous sandwiches the next day.

1 3-pound top sirloin steak
   1-1/4 inches thick
2 tablespoons black peppercorns,
   crushed
1 teaspoon butter
1/2 cup dry white wine
1 tablespoon brandy
1 tablespoon butter (optional)

Makes 6 servings
Each serving, 1 slice 1x3x1/4 inches,
contains:
   1/2 Fat Exchange
   1 Low-fat Meat Exchange
   78 calories

1-1/2 pounds sirloin steak
1 tablespoon butter
1 cup sliced, fresh mushrooms
   (1/4 pound)
1 cup sliced onion
2-1/2 tablespoons flour
2-1/2 cups beef stock
1 tablespoon TOMATO JUICE
   CATSUP, page 70
1/2 teaspoon paprika
1/2 teaspoon sweet basil
1/4 teaspoon nutmeg
3 tablespoons sherry
3/4 cup sour cream

Makes 6 servings
Each serving contains:
   3 Low-fat Meat Exchanges
   1-1/2 Fat Exchanges
   233 calories
1/2 cup rice or noodles contains:
   1 Bread Exchange
   70 calories

BEEF STROGANOFF

Trim all fat from the meat and cut it into narrow strips. In a heavy iron skillet melt 2 teaspoons of the butter. Add the sliced mushrooms and onions; cook until tender and lightly browned. Remove mushrooms and onions and put them in a bowl. Do not wash the pan. In the same pan melt the remaining teaspoon of butter. Add the meat and lightly brown it on all sides. Put the meat in the bowl with the mushrooms and onions.

Add the flour to the skillet and brown it with the remaining butter (there won't be much!). In a saucepan bring the BEEF STOCK to a boil and add slowly to the flour mixture, stirring constantly to form a smooth sauce.

Add the TOMATO JUICE CATSUP, paprika, basil, nutmeg and sherry. Simmer the sauce for 10 minutes. Return the meat, mushrooms and onions to the pan and simmer for 10 more minutes. Add the sour cream and serve immediately.

I like to serve Beef Stroganoff with thinly sliced rye bread, lightly spread with cream cheese and sprinkled with paprika.

You can cut the Fat Exchange in the Beef Stroganoff by adding 1/2 cup sour cream mixed with 1/4 cup plain yogurt.

Many people like Beef Stroganoff served over rice or noodles. If you serve it over either rice or noodles, remember: 1/2 cup rice or noodles contains 1 Bread Exchange and 70 calories.

SHISH KEBAB

Combine all ingredients for the marinade sauce and marinate lamb cubes for 8 hours.

Wash green pepper and cut in 1-inch squares removing all seeds and veins. Peel onions and parboil for 3 minutes. Arrange cubes of marinated lamb on skewers alternating the lamb with the cherry tomatoes, green pepper and the onions. Put the skewers back in the marinade for 1 or 2 hours. Then broil in the oven or on a charcoal fire until the lamb is cooked the desired amount. Some people like pink lamb; others prefer it well-done.

1 pound lean lamb, cut in cubes
1 green bell pepper
12 small boiling onions
12 cherry tomatoes

MARINADE SAUCE
1/2 cup red wine vinegar
2 tablespoons soy sauce
1/4 teaspoon freshly ground
   black pepper
dash cayenne pepper
1 teaspoon salt
1/2 cup minced onion
1 tablespoon oregano

Makes 6 servings
Each serving contains:
   2 Low-fat Meat Exchanges
   1 Vegetable Exchange
   135 calories

1-1/2 pounds lean beef, cut in
   1-inch cubes
1/2 cup flour
4 teaspoons butter
2 leeks, white part only, sliced
2 cups sliced fresh mushrooms
   (1/2 pound)
2 sprigs parsley, minced
1 bud garlic, pressed
1 bay leaf (remove when cooked)
1/2 teaspoon thyme
1/2 teaspoon dill weed
1/2 teaspoon summer savory
1 teaspoon salt
1/2 teaspoon freshly ground
   black pepper
1-1/2 cups water
2 cups dry red wine
1 carrot, sliced
2 turnips, cut in large pieces
10 small boiling onions,
   peeled and whole
2 cups green peas

Makes 8 servings
Each serving contains:
   2 Low-fat Meat Exchanges
   1 Vegetable Exchange
   1/2 Fat Exchange
   1/4 Bread Exchange
   176 calories

JONES STEW

Put cubed beef and flour in paper bag and shake until the meat is thoroughly coated. Melt butter in bottom of a heavy soup kettle, then add leeks and mushrooms. Sauté until tender and remove from pan. Do not wash pan. Add the meat to the hot pan and brown rapidly. When meat is brown, return leeks and mushrooms to pan. Add parsley and all other spices. Next add 1/2 cup water and 1 cup of the wine. Simmer, covered, for 1 hour. Then add remaining 1 cup of water and 1 cup of wine, and simmer 1/2 hour. At this point, cool and refrigerate overnight. Chip off all fat from the top. When reheating bring to a slow boil and add all vegetables except peas. Simmer, covered, for 1 hour more. Add peas and cook until they are tender, about 10 minutes.

1 pound lean pork roast, cooked
   (4 cups cubed)
1 20-ounce can (2 cups) unsweetened
   pineapple chunks with juice
2 tablespoons cornstarch
1/2 teaspoon salt
1/3 cup cider vinegar
3 tablespoons fructose
1 tablespoon soy sauce
1 cup sliced fresh mushrooms
   (1/4 pound)
1/2 green bell pepper, thinly sliced
1/2 onion, thinly sliced
1 6-ounce can water chestnuts,
   thinly sliced

Makes 8 servings
Each serving contains:
   2 Low-fat Meat Exchanges
   1 Fruit Exchange
   1/2 Vegetable Exchange
   163 calories
1/2 cup cooked white rice contains:
   1 Bread Exchange
   70 calories

SWEET AND SOUR PORK

Cut the roast pork in 1-inch cubes, making sure to remove all fat. It is easier to remove the fat and cut the pork when it is cold, and this is a marvelous way to use leftover pork roast. Drain the juice from the pineapple chunks and pour it in a large saucepan. Add cornstarch, salt and vinegar and cook, stirring constantly, until the sauce has thickened. Add fructose, soy sauce, pineapple chunks and meat. Let mixture stand for one hour. Then add the mushrooms, bell pepper, onion and water chestnuts. Cook until the vegetables are done, but still slightly crisp. Serve over plain white, cooked rice.

Try serving the pork with Chinese pea pods. Start with egg flower soup.

ORIENTAL BEEF AND PEA PODS

Slice flank steak diagonally across the grain in 1/2-inch strips. Brown the meat strips in a heavy iron skillet in hot oil and then remove from skillet. Do not wash pan. Cook the bean sprouts, pea pods, green onions and mushrooms in the same skillet just a few minutes, until crunchy-tender. Add the BEEF STOCK, soy sauce and ginger. Cover and cook for 2 minutes. Stir in the cornstarch mixed with cold water and salt. Cook, stirring, until clear and slightly thickened. Add meat strips and mix well. Serve over white rice.

1 pound flank steak
1 tablespoon oil
1/2 pound bean sprouts
1/2 pound Chinese pea pods
1 cup chopped green onions
2 cups sliced fresh mushrooms
1 cup beef stock
3 tablespoons soy sauce
1 teaspoon peeled, grated ginger root
1-1/2 tablespoons cornstarch
2 tablespoons cold water
1/2 teaspoon salt

Makes 6 servings
Each serving contains:
    2 Low-fat Meat Exchanges
    1/2 Fat Exchange
    1-1/4 Vegetable Exchanges
    164 calories
1/2 cup cooked white rice contains:
    1 Bread Exchange
    70 calories

1 pound sliced bacon

1 slice bacon contains:
1 Fat Exchange
45 calories
1 teaspoon bacon fat contains:
1 Fat Exchange
45 calories

BAKED BACON

Use a broiler pan or a rack over a pan so that the fat can drip through while the bacon is cooking. Place the bacon slices side by side on the broiler pan and bake at 350° for 15 minutes. Remove the bacon and drain on paper towels. Repeat procedure, as only 1/2 pound of bacon will fit on the broiler pan at one time. Store baked bacon in the refrigerator until needed. To heat, put the baked bacon in a pan in a 300° oven for about 5 minutes, or until it is desired crispness. The bacon is much less fatty than fried bacon and much easier and faster to prepare in the morning, or whenever you want just a slice or two of bacon.

CORNED BEEF AND CABBAGE

Put the corned beef in a big saucepan or soup kettle and cover it with cold water. Add all of the other ingredients, except the vegetables, and bring water to a boil. Reduce the heat to a slow boil or simmer. Simmer for 3 hours or 1 hour per pound of corned beef.

At this point STOP! Refrigerate overnight and remove all fat from the top.

When cooking the next day, bring to a slow boil and add potatoes, carrots and celery. Cook for 1/2 hour or until vegetables are tender. During the last 15 minutes of cooking time add the cabbage. Do not overcook the cabbage.

I would rather let someone else eat the potatoes and have hot rye bread.

3 to 4 pounds of lean corned beef
2 garlic buds cut in half
1 onion, chopped
2 bay leaves
10 peppercorns
2 tablespoons pickling spices
3 potatoes, quartered
6 small carrots, halved
4 stalks celery, cut in pieces
1 head cabbage, quartered

Makes 6 servings
Each serving contains:
   1 Medium-fat Meat Exchange
      (1 slice corned beef 2 x 3 x
      1/8 inch)
   1 Bread Exchange
   1 Vegetable Exchange
   170 calories (add 75 calories for
      each additional Medium-fat
      Meat Exchange)

meat/poultry

1 pound ground beef (round)
1 cup chopped onion
1 pound spinach, chopped
2 eggs, lightly beaten
1/2 teaspoon salt

Makes 4 servings
Each serving contains:
   3 Medium-fat Meat Exchanges
   1 Vegetable Exchange
   250 calories

POPEYE'S SPINACH HASH

Put ground beef in a cured, heavy skillet. Add the chopped onion and cook until meat is done and onion is tender. Cook spinach and drain thoroughly in a strainer until completely dry. Add chopped spinach to meat mixture and mix well. Add lightly beaten eggs and salt. Stir until egg is completely cooked.

CHILI CON CARNE

Cut all fat off meat and cut it in 1/2-inch cubes. Put the meat in a hot, cured, heavy iron skillet and brown. Then remove meat from skillet and set aside. Do not wash pan. Put onions, garlic and imitation bacon bits into a hot skillet and cook until onions are clear and slightly browned. Mix the chili powder and flour together in a bowl. Add enough juice from the canned tomatoes to make a paste. Add the paste to the onions and put in a large saucepan with a lid. Add the meat and the canned tomatoes with the remaining tomato juice. Simmer for 1/2 hour. Add the bay leaves, salt, oregano, red wine vinegar and fructose. Cover and simmer for 2 hours.

If you are using beans, add them the last 15 minutes of cooking time.

2 pounds lean round steak
4 cups sliced onion
4 garlic buds, minced
2 tablespoons imitation bacon bits
4 tablespoons chili powder
1 tablespoon flour
1 28-ounce can tomatoes, coarsely chopped
juice from canned tomatoes
3 bay leaves
1 tablespoon salt
1 tablespoon oregano
1 tablespoon red wine vinegar
2 teaspoons fructose
2 cups canned red kidney beans (optional)

Makes 8 servings
Each serving contains:
   3 Low-fat Meat Exchanges
   1 Vegetable Exchange
   190 calories
With beans, add:
   1/2 Bread Exchange
   35 calories

1 large pre-cooked, smoked ham
1 20-ounce can unsweetened
    pineapple rings
whole cloves, at least 30

1 slice (2 x 3 x 1/8 inches)
contains:
    1 Low-fat Meat Exchange
    55 calories

HOLIDAY HAM

Preheat the oven to 500°. Cut the skin, not the fat, off of the ham, except at the very ends over the bone.

Put the ham in preheated oven until the fat is well-browned, about 15 minutes. Remove the ham and turn the oven down to 200°. Place the pineapple rings all over the top of the ham, securing them with toothpicks. Stick whole cloves all over the ham, about 1 inch apart.

Put the ham back in the oven and bake at 200° all day—or until you are ready to serve it. As long as it stays in the oven for at least 4 hours, it will be delicious. You can leave it for as long as 8 hours without hurting it. Baste frequently.

HAM SLICES IN ORANGE SAUCE

Trim all the fat from the ham slices. Sprinkle both sides of each slice with paprika. In a cured, heavy iron skillet, lightly brown the ham on both sides.

In a saucepan, mix the cornstarch with the orange juice. Add the salt, cinnamon, fructose, grated orange peel and cloves. Cook over low heat until clear and slightly thickened. Pour the orange sauce over the ham slices and garnish with the orange slices.

This is excellent served with WILD RICE AND SESAME SEEDS , page 157.

4 slices cooked ham
paprika
1-1/2 teaspoons cornstarch
1/2 cup orange juice
1/4 teaspoon salt
1/4 teaspoon cinnamon
2 tablespoons fructose
2 teaspoons grated orange peel
10 whole cloves
1 orange, thinly sliced

Makes 4 servings
Each serving contains:
   2 Low-fat Meat Exchanges (depend-
     ing on size of ham slices)
   1 Fruit Exchange
   150 calories

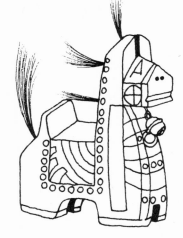

4 large, fresh green chilis (or 4 large, canned, whole green chilis)
1 large green apple
1/4 pound ground beef (round)
1/2 teaspoon salt
2 eggs, separated
4 teaspoons flour, sifted
chopped parsley, for garnish
pomegranate seeds, for garnish

CHEESE SAUCE

1 cup crumbled hoop or farmer cheese
1 cup whole milk
1/8 teaspoon cinnamon
3/4 teaspoon fructose

Makes 4 servings
Each serving contains:
  2-1/4 Medium-fat Meat Exchanges
  1/4 Whole Milk Exchange
  1/4 Fruit Exchange
  1/2 Vegetable Exchange
  233 calories

CHILIS RELLENOS WITH CHEESE SAUCE

To make the sauce put all the ingredients in a blender and blend until smooth. Allow to stand at room temperature for 1 hour before serving.

When using fresh chilis, split each one lengthwise. Very carefully remove all of the seeds and veins from each chili; then dry them. Place chilis on a cookie sheet and put them under the broiler until brown and crinkly on both sides. Wrap the broiled chilis in a wet cloth for 10 minutes. Remove them from the cloth. Carefully remove the blistered skins completely.

To prepare canned chilis, it is necessary only to remove the seeds and veins.

Peel, core and chop the apple into 1/4-inch cubes. Crumble the ground beef and mix it with the apple and salt. Cook the meat until it is done but not browned. Fill each chili with 1/4 of the meat mixture. Place the chilis on a slightly oiled or Teflon cookie sheet. Sprinkle 1 teaspoon flour over the top of the chilis and rub it all over the top surface. Beat the egg whites until they are stiff but not dry. Beat the yolks and fold them into the whites. Spoon 1/4 of the egg mixture over each chili. Put the chilis under the broiler until lightly browned. Then put them in a 350° oven for 10 minutes. To serve, pour 1/4 of the cheese sauce over each chili and garnish it with chopped parsley and a few pomegranate seeds.

Serve with hot tortillas or MEXICAN RICE.

LASAGNA

In a large saucepan, simmer canned tomatoes, chopped and without juice, tomato paste, parsley, salt, pepper, oregano, thyme and marjoram for 1/2 hour.

In a hot, heavy iron skillet, sauté meat until done. Add to tomato sauce. Do not wash pan. Put onion and garlic in the same pan and cook until onion is clear and slightly brown. Add to tomato sauce and continue to simmer sauce for another 1/2 hour.

While the sauce is simmering, cook the lasagna in 3 quarts of boiling, salted water for about 12 minutes. Drain and rinse with cold water in a colander.

Cover the bottom of a large, flat baking dish with 1/4 inch of the meat sauce. Add a layer of lasagna, trimming edges to fit the dish. On top of this put a layer of ricotta cheese, then a layer of mozzarella cheese, and finally sprinkle with Parmesan cheese. Repeat layers until the baking dish is filled. Top layer should be meat sauce sprinkled with Parmesan cheese.

Bake at 350° for 45 minutes.

2 20-ounce cans solid-pack tomatoes
4 6-ounce cans Italian tomato paste
1 large bunch parsley, chopped
1 teaspoon salt
1/2 teaspoon freshly ground
    black pepper
2 teaspoons oregano
1/2 teaspoon thyme
1/2 teaspoon marjoram
2 pounds lean ground sirloin
4 large onions, chopped
2 buds garlic, minced or pressed
1/2 pound lasagna
1 pound ricotta cheese
1/2 pound mozzarella cheese
1/4 pound Parmesan cheese

Makes 16 servings
Each serving contains:
    3 Low-fat Meat Exchanges
    1/2 Bread Exchange
    1 Vegetable Exchange
    225 calories

3 whole boned chicken breasts
1/2 cup flour in a paper bag with
  salt and freshly ground pepper
1 tablespoon butter
1 cup beef stock
1/2 cup Burgundy
1 teaspoon thyme
1 teaspoon marjoram
2 tablespoons chopped parsley
12 small, white boiling onions,
  peeled
4 celery stalks, whole

Makes 6 servings
Each serving contains:
  2 Low-fat Meat Exchanges
  1/2 Vegetable Exchange
  1/2 Fat Exchange
  146 calories

COQ AU VIN
(Chicken in Burgundy)

Cut chicken breasts in half, put in the bag of flour and shake until well coated. Brown the chicken breasts in butter. Heat the beef stock and add to the pan. Add wine, thyme, marjoram, parsley, and onions. Cover with celery stalks. Cook slowly for 1 hour over low heat. Discard celery stalks and remove chicken and onions to a serving dish. Simmer gravy until reduced slightly. Spoon the sauce over the chicken and onions.

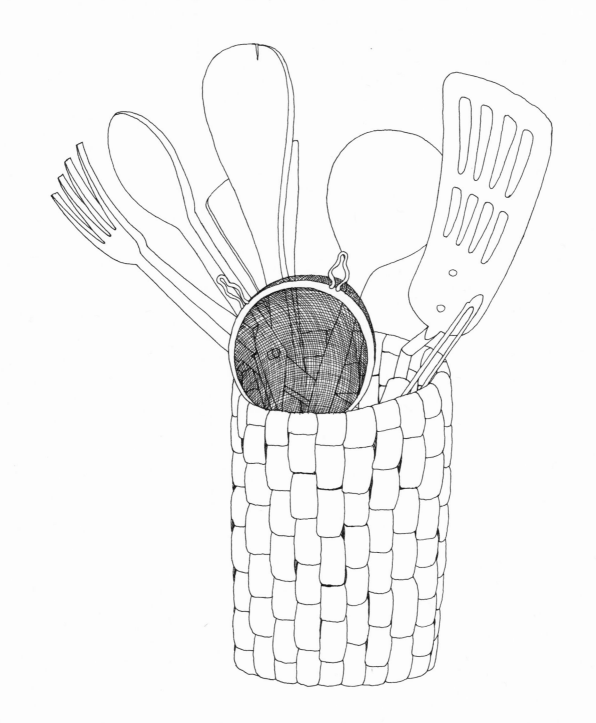

3 cups BASIC WHITE SAUCE,
   page 55
1/2 teaspoon salt
1/4 teaspoon white pepper
1/4 teaspoon nutmeg
2 teaspoons olive oil
3 tablespoons minced onion
3 tablespoons finely chopped celery
3 tablespoons finely chopped carrot
2 tablespoons minced parsley
2 cups finely chopped, cooked
   chicken
3/4 teaspoon salt
1/4 teaspoon oregano
1/4 teaspoon sweet basil
1/2 teaspoon white pepper
3/4 cup dry white wine
8 CREPES, page 145
1/4 cup tomato sauce
1/4 cup whole milk
1/2 cup Parmesan cheese

Makes 8 servings
Each serving contains:
   3/4 Bread Exchange
   1-1/2 Low-fat Meat Exchanges
   1 Fat Exchange
   1/2 Whole Milk Exchange
   264 calories

CHICKEN CANNELONI

Make the BASIC WHITE SAUCE doubling the recipe. Add salt, white pepper and nutmeg to the sauce and mix well. Set aside.

Heat olive oil in a cured iron skillet. Add the onion, celery, carrot and parsley. Sauté for 15 minutes or until the vegetables are tender.

Add chicken, salt, oregano, sweet basil, white pepper and white wine. Simmer until the wine is reduced by half. Remove from heat, add 1-1/2 cups of the BASIC WHITE SAUCE to the chicken mixture and mix well.

Heat the crepes so they are pliable. Divide the chicken mixture equally on the crepes and roll each one around the filling, placing it folded side down in a flat Teflon baking dish.

To the remaining 1-1/2 cups of BASIC WHITE SAUCE, add the tomato sauce and milk. Mix well and pour evenly over the stuffed crepes. Sprinkle each with 1 tablespoon Parmesan cheese.

Bake at 425° for 10 minutes or until the tops are lightly browned.

CHICKEN JEANNO

In a heavy iron skillet, heat 2 tablespoons butter and 1 tablespoon olive oil. Add the minced garlic and the grated carrots, and cook for 3 minutes.

Add the minced onions and parsley, and sauté until all of the vegetables are tender. Add the canned tomatoes and juice. Add the tomato paste and simmer, uncovered, for 1/2 hour. Add oregano, salt and pepper, and simmer 1/2 hour longer.

While the sauce is cooking, shake each chicken breast in a brown paper bag containing the flour, salt and pepper until lightly coated. In a large, cured skillet, put 2 teaspoons butter and 1 teaspoon olive oil and heat. Add the chicken breasts and sauté until golden brown and fork tender.

When the sauce is cooked, arrange the chicken breasts on top of the sauce, first covering with the grated mozzarella cheese. Then sprinkle grated Parmesan on top. Cover the pan and heat slowly until all the cheese is melted.

2 tablespoons butter
1 tablespoon olive oil
2 garlic buds, minced
4 small carrots, peeled and grated
1 cup minced onion
1/4 cup minced parsley
2 cups Italian tomatoes, chopped,
   plus the juice from the can
1 6-ounce can tomato paste
1 teaspoon oregano
1/2 teaspoon salt
1/4 teaspoon freshly ground black pepper
4 whole chicken breasts, boned,
   skinned and cut in half
1/2 cup flour
1/2 teaspoon salt
1/4 teaspoon pepper
2 teaspoons more butter
1 teaspoon more olive oil
1-3/4 cups grated mozzarella cheese
   (or Monterey Jack cheese)
1/4 cup grated Parmesan cheese

Makes 8 servings
Each serving contains:
   3 Medium-fat Meat Exchanges
   1-1/2 Fat Exchanges
   1-1/2 Vegetable Exchanges
   331 calories

meat/poultry

whole roasting chickens
salt

1 slice, 3 x 2 x 1/8 inch or 1 ounce
or 1/4 cup, chopped, contains:
    1 Low-fat Meat Exchange
    55 calories

1 turkey
1 tablespoon oil
salt

1 slice, 3 x 2 x 1/8 inch, without
skin, or 1 ounce or 1/4 cup,
chopped, contains:
    1 Low-fat Meat Exchange
    55 calories

ROAST CHICKEN

Preheat oven to 350°.

Put the chickens breast-side down in a flat roasting pan and salt them.

Bake at 350° for about 1 hour or until the liquid runs clear.

If you are going to use the chickens for salad, allow them to cool until they can easily be handled. Remove all skin and cut the meat from the bones. Refrigerate before cutting into smaller pieces.

ROAST TURKEY

Preheat the oven to 325°. Put the turkey, **breast down,** in a flat roasting pan. Rub the turkey with oil and salt. Put it in the oven and cook for 20 minutes per pound.

Take the turkey out of the oven, allow it to cool slightly and put it on a platter. Pour the turkey drippings into a bowl and put it in the freezer. When the fat has solidified on the top (about 30 minutes) scrape it off and use the DEFATTED DRIPPINGS for gravy with your turkey dinner or store them in the refrigerator to use in your TURKEY SOUP!

Bread rarely comes to mind when thinking of diets; few people ever think of bread alone. I think of it generously spread with butter, mayonnaise or maybe jam.

Bread is a wholesome food and certain amounts of it are necessary for good nutrition. However, bread could become a rather dreary part of a diet if you always had to eat it "plain" without anything on it.

I have given you several recipes to help make your required Bread Exchanges delightful additions to your daily meals.

breads pancakes and such

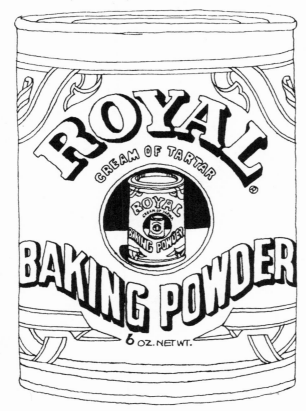

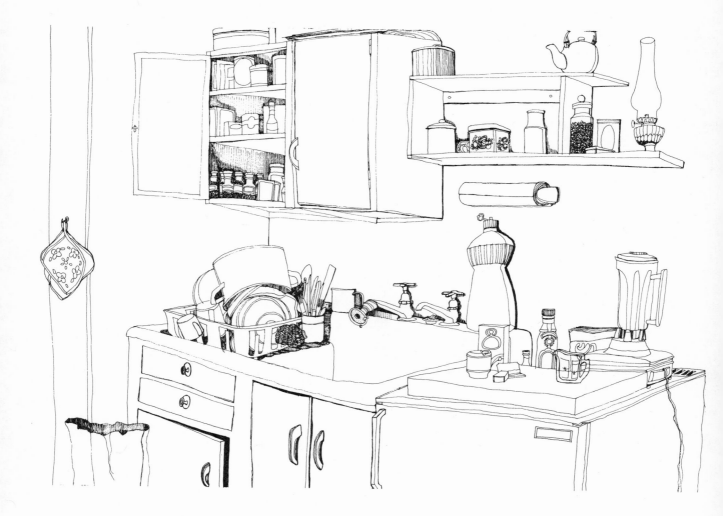

ONION-DILL BREAD

Soften yeast in 1/4 cup warm water. Warm cottage cheese in saucepan. Add yeast in water to the warm cottage cheese. Add fructose, minced onion, soda, beaten egg, dill seed and salt. Mix well. Add the sifted flour, a little at a time, mixing well. Cover and allow to stand at room temperature for several hours, or until doubled in bulk. Stir dough until again reduced to original size, and put it in a well-oiled, standard-sized metal loaf pan. Cover the loaf pan and allow the dough to again double in bulk. Bake in a 350° oven for 40 minutes.

This bread is delicious right from the oven. However, it's much easier to slice when cool. Wrap sliced bread in foil and store in the refrigerator until ready to use. Then warm in the oven before serving.

1 yeast cake or 1 package dry yeast
1/4 cup warm water
1/2 pint small curd cottage cheese
4 teaspoons fructose
1/4 cup minced onion
1/4 teaspoon baking soda
1 egg, lightly beaten
2 tablespoons dill seed
1 teaspoon salt
2 cups all-purpose flour

Makes 18 slices
Each slice contains:
    1 Bread Exchange
    70 calories

RYE BREAD

Soften yeast in 1/4 cup warm water. Warm cottage cheese in saucepan. Add yeast in water to the warm cottage cheese. Add fructose, soda, beaten egg, caraway seeds and salt. Mix well. Add the flour a little at a time, mixing well. Cover and allow to stand at room temperature for several hours, or until doubled in bulk. Stir dough until reduced to original size, and put in a well-oiled, standard-size metal loaf pan. Cover the loaf pan and again allow dough to double in bulk. Bake in a 350° oven for 1 hour.

When the bread is cool, slice and lightly butter each slice. Wrap in foil and warm before serving. Excellent served hot with cold meat, poultry or seafood.

1 yeast cake or 1 package dry yeast
1/4 cup warm water
1/2 pint small curd cottage cheese
4 teaspoons fructose
1/4 teaspoon baking soda
1 egg, lightly beaten
2 tablespoons caraway seeds
1 teaspoon salt
1 cup all-purpose flour
1 cup rye flour

Makes 16 slices
Each slice contains:
    1 Bread Exchange
    70 calories

breads

6 tablespoons corn oil margarine
2 cups less 2 tablespoons all-purpose
   flour
1/8 teaspoon salt
1-1/2 teaspoons baking soda
1/2 cup fructose
2 eggs, lightly beaten
1/2 cup buttermilk
1 teaspoon vanilla extract
3 ripe bananas, mashed with a fork

Makes 18 slices
Each slice contains:
   1 Bread Exchange
   1 Fat Exchange
   3/4 Fruit Exchange
   145 calories

1 yeast cake or 1 package dry yeast
1/4 cup warm water
1 cup cottage cheese, warmed
1 egg, lightly beaten
4 teaspoons fructose
1/4 teaspoon baking soda
1 teaspoon salt
3 tablespoons TOASTED SESAME
   SEEDS, page 181
2 cups all-purpose flour

Makes 20 thin slices
Each slice contains:
   1 Bread Exchange
   1/4 Fat Exchange
   81 calories

BANANA BREAD

Allow margarine to come to room temperature so that it is soft. Cream the margarine and 1/2 of the flour, mixed with the salt, soda and fructose. Add the beaten eggs and mix well. Add the remaining flour and buttermilk alternately. Then add the vanilla and the mashed bananas. Put the dough in a standard-size metal loaf pan which has been greased with part of the margarine (I always use what is left on the wrapper). Then shake a little flour around in the pan until all sides are coated and pour the flour out. Bake at 350° for 1 hour and 15 minutes. Cool the bread on its side. When cool, wrap the bread in aluminum foil or put it in a tight plastic bag in the refrigerator. If possible keep it for 2 days before eating it. To serve, slice the bread thinly, wrap tightly in foil and put it in a 300° oven for about 10 minutes or until it is hot. If you can spare the Fat Exchange, butter the banana bread before reheating it.

SESAME TOAST

Proceed exactly as you do for ONION-DILL BREAD, adding sesame seeds before adding flour.

When bread is cooked, cool it to room temperature and put in the refrigerator for several hours. It is easier to slice thinly when it is cold. Slice very thinly (20 slices to a standard-size loaf pan, 5-1/2x9-1/2x3 inches. Put slices side-by-side on a cookie sheet and put under the broiler until golden brown. Turn each slice over and brown on the other side. Place the toast on cake racks to cool. Serve with soup, salad or any time you want an interesting and different bread exchange. I love Sesame Toast with curry.

You may be wondering why this recipe is called Sesame Toast. I think the toast is so fabulous that it is worth making the bread just to be able to toast it.

TOASTED TORTILLA TRIANGLES

12 corn tortillas
salt

6 Tortilla Triangles contain:
   1 Bread Exchange
   70 calories

Cut each tortilla into 6 pie-shaped pieces. Place 1/2 of the tortilla triangles on a cookie sheet, spread out, and salt lightly. Bake them in a 400° oven for 10 minutes. Remove from oven, turn each one over and return them to the 400° oven for 3 more minutes. Place second half of tortilla triangles on cookie sheet and repeat process.

Toasted Tortilla Triangles are marvelous to serve with dips, with salads and soups, or crumbled up in casserole dishes. I use them as the base of my TOSTADA SALAD on page 92.

If you prefer smaller chips, cut the tortillas into smaller triangles before toasting them. They are so much fresher-tasting than the tortilla chips you buy at the store and more importantly they are fat free.

Variations: Sprinkle the tortillas with seasoned salts, cumin and chili powder for different flavors.

CROUTONS

4 slices old bread

Makes 2 cups Croutons
1/2 cup Croutons contains:
   1 Bread Exchange
   70 calories

If you have no old bread, separate slices of fresh bread and leave them on a countertop for several hours, turning occasionally, until they can be cut up easily.

Slice the bread in 1/4-inch squares. Place squares in a large, shallow pan or a cookie sheet, and put in a 300° oven for 20 minutes, or until a golden brown. Turn a few times so squares will brown evenly.

breads

2 eggs
1/4 teaspoon baking soda
1/4 teaspoon salt
2-1/2 teaspoons baking powder
1 cup buttermilk
1 cup all-purpose flour
1 teaspoon butter

Makes 20 3-inch pancakes
2 pancakes contain:
   1 Bread Exchange
   70 calories

4 eggs, separated
1 cup creamed-style cottage cheese
1/4 cup all-purpose flour
1/4 teaspoon salt
1 teaspoon butter

Makes 8 5-inch pancakes
Each pancake contains:
   1 Medium-fat Meat Exchange
   1/4 Bread Exchange
   93 calories

MY PANCAKES

Beat the eggs, soda, salt and baking powder together until frothy. Add the buttermilk and flour. Mix well. Heat a cured iron skillet or Teflon pan. Add butter and allow it to melt as the pan heats. When the pan is hot, wipe the butter out with a paper towel. Use a soup ladle to pour out the batter and cook the pancakes over moderate heat.

Variations: Add 1/8 teaspoon dry mustard to the batter and serve the pancakes spread with sour cream, cinnamon and a little fructose sprinkled on top. This is nice with sliced, baked apples for breakfast, and broiled Canadian bacon.

PUFFY PANCAKES

Beat the egg whites until they are stiff, but not dry. Transfer the beater to the yolks (this maneuver saves washing the beater in between). Beat the yolks until they are light in color. Beat the cottage cheese, flour and salt into the egg yolks. Carefully fold in the beaten egg whites. Use either a cured iron skillet or a Teflon pan. Add a teaspoon of butter and let it melt as the pan heats. Then wipe the butter out of the pan with a paper towel and pour the batter into the hot pan with a soup ladle. Cook over moderate heat until completely cooked on the first side. Very carefully turn the pancakes over. They are fragile and light as a feather and delicious!

I make these ahead of time, as they freeze beautifully. Before serving them thaw completely and heat, wrapped in foil, in a 300° oven for 15 minutes.

I love to serve these pancakes with sour cream and STRAW-BERRY JAM, page 73.

CREPES

Put milk, flour and salt in a bowl and beat with an egg beater until well mixed. Beat in the eggs and mix well.

In a cured iron omelette or crepe pan, melt 1/2 teaspoon butter. When the butter is melted and the pan is hot, tilt the pan to make sure the entire pan is buttered. Pour in just enough crepe batter to barely cover the bottom of the pan (about 2 tablespoons) and tilt the pan from side to side to spread the batter evenly. When the edges start to curl, carefully turn the crêpe with a spatula and brown the other side.

To keep the crepes pliable, put them in a covered casserole in a warm oven as you make them.

To Freeze: I often make crepes and freeze them. Put a piece of aluminum foil between each crepe and wrap them well so that they are not exposed to the air. Before using, bring to room temperature and put them in a 300° oven for 20 minutes so they are soft and pliable. Otherwise they will break when you try to fold them.

1 cup milk
3/4 cup all-purpose flour
1/4 teaspoon salt
2 eggs, lightly beaten
1/2 teaspoon butter

Makes 8 crêpes
Each crêpe contains:
   1/2 Bread Exchange
   1/4 Medium-fat Meat Exchange
   53 calories

POPOVERS

Put eggs, milk, sifted flour and salt in a bowl and beat until frothy, about 1-1/2 minutes. Add the oil and beat for 30 seconds more. Do not overbeat. Pour the batter into 8 oiled custard cups or muffin tins. Bake in a 475° oven for 15 minutes. Reduce oven heat to 350° and bake for 30 minutes more, or until firm and well browned. A few minutes before the popovers are completely cooked, pierce the top of each one with a sharp knife, letting the steam escape.

If you prefer your popovers dry on the inside, leave them in a cool oven, with the door ajar, for 20 minutes or so after they are cooked.

Try filling a popover with INSTANT CUSTARD for a cream puff.

2 eggs
1 cup milk
1 cup all-purpose flour
1/2 teaspoon salt
2 teaspoons salad oil

Makes 8 popovers
Each popover contains:
   1 Bread Exchange
   70 calories

145

breads

2 eggs, separated
1/2 cup yogurt
3/4 cup all-purpose flour
1/4 teaspoon salt
2 teaspoons baking powder
2 teaspoons melted butter or
   margarine

Makes 4 servings
1 4-inch waffle contains:
  1 Bread Exchange
  1/2 Fat Exchange
  93 calories

WAFFLES

Beat egg whites until stiff. Put the yogurt, egg yolks, flour, salt, baking powder and butter in the blender and mix until smooth. Pour blended mixture into a bowl and gently fold in the beaten egg whites. Cook in a preheated Teflon waffle iron, or lightly oil regular waffle iron.

Try spreading each waffle with 2 tablespoons (1 Fat Exchange) sour cream and CITRUS SAUCE COMPOTE.

YORKSHIRE PUDDING

Pour hot DEFATTED BEEF DRIPPINGS into a pan 11x7x1-1/2 inches. Pour POPOVER batter into the pan over the hot drippings. Bake at 450° for 25 minutes. Cut into 8 sections and serve at once. Marvelous served with roast beef.

1/4 cup hot DEFATTED BEEF
    DRIPPINGS, page 52
1 full recipe for POPOVERS, page 145

Makes 8 servings
Each serving contains:
    1 Bread Exchange
    70 calories

NOODLES ROMANOV

Cook and drain the noodles. Mix together all other ingredients, except the Parmesan cheese, and fold into the cooked noodles. Put noodles in a casserole and sprinkle with Parmesan cheese. Bake at 350° for 30 minutes.

This is a marvelous side dish for cold meats. I also like to serve it with broiled meat and poultry.

1 8-ounce package noodles
1/2 pint sour cream
1/2 pint cottage cheese
1/4 cup finely chopped parsley
1/4 cup finely chopped chives
    or green onion tops
2 tablespoons Worcestershire sauce
1/2 teaspoon salt
4 drops Tabasco sauce
2 tablespoons grated Parmesan cheese
    cheese

Makes 8 servings
Each serving contains:
    1 Bread Exchange
    1 Fat Exchange
    1/2 Low-fat Meat Exchange
    143 calories

breads

2 eggs, separated
1-1/2 cups water
1 teaspoon salt
1 cup cornmeal
1 tablespoon butter
1 cup buttermilk

Makes 8 servings
Each serving contains:
   1 Bread Exchange
   1/4 Medium-fat Meat Exchange
   93 calories

1 egg
3/4 cup all-purpose flour
1/2 teaspoon salt
1/3 cup CHICKEN BOUILLON,
   page 44, for batter
1-1/2 to 2 quarts CHICKEN
   BOUILLON, for cooking

Makes 12 dumplings
4 dumplings contain:
   1-1/4 Bread Exchanges
   1/4 Medium-fat Meat Exchange
   107 calories

SPOON BREAD

Beat egg whites until stiff, but not dry. Bring water and salt to a boil. Gradually stir in the cornmeal. When the mixture is smooth remove the pan from heat. Add the butter and stir it in. Beat the egg yolk and add to the cornmeal mixture. Add buttermilk and beat until smooth. Beat the egg whites until stiff and carefully fold them into the batter. Pour the batter into an oiled casserole. Bake at 400° for about 30 minutes. Spoon from casserole onto the plates. I love this with SKINNY CHICKEN GRAVY!

TEXAS DUMPLINGS

Beat the egg with a wire whisk. Slowly beat in the flour, salt and chicken bouillon. Beat until well mixed and smooth. In a large pot, boil 1-1/2 to 2 quarts of chicken bouillon (or water to which a little chicken stock has been added). Drop the dumplings by the teaspoonful into the boiling bouillon and cook uncovered for 10 minutes.

vegetables

For a diet program calling for so many vegetables, you may at first think this section is too short. However, I have purposely kept it that way.

Probably the most important reason for this is that I prefer almost all vegetables raw, and therefore I have a very large salad section.

When cooking vegetables, I think they are best steamed "just done" or what I call crisp tender. This is a very simple but delicious and nutritious way to serve them. Also, they are prettier because they retain their natural color.

If you wish more elaborate vegetable dishes, just add sauces to your steamed vegetables. For example: put HAPPY HOLLANDAISE SAUCE on steamed broccoli, CHEDDAR CHEESE SAUCE on steamed cauliflower, MORNAY SAUCE on steamed asparagus, MUSTARD SAUCE on steamed cabbage, and SKINNY GRAVIES on potatoes, carrots and turnips.

Another interesting way of using cooked vegetables is to serve them cold with CREAMY TARRAGON DRESSING, HORSERADISH DRESSING, CURRY DRESSING or any other dressing you particularly like. Still another variation: marinate vegetables overnight in FRENCH or ITALIAN DRESSING. Use your imagination!

vegetables

1 8-ounce can button mushrooms
2 buds garlic, peeled and halved
2 tablespoons olive oil
4 teaspoons red wine vinegar
1 teaspoon Worcestershire sauce
1 drop Tabasco sauce
1/8 teaspoon salt

Makes 1 cup
1/4 cup contains:
   1/2 Vegetable Exchange
   13 calories

MARINATED MUSHROOMS

Open and drain mushrooms, reserving liquid. Place 1/2 of the mushrooms in a glass jar and put one bud of garlic cut in half on top of them. Add remaining mushrooms and put another halved bud of garlic on top. Mix all other ingredients together and pour over mushrooms. Add enough of the liquid from the mushrooms to cover them. Shake jar to mix well and store in the refrigerator. Allow mushrooms to marinate 24 hours before serving.

Serve as hors d'oeuvre. Put a toothpick in each mushroom and serve on a plate or in a shallow bowl.

CAPONATA ANTIPASTO
(Cold Eggplant Appetizer)

Put 1 tablespoon olive oil in a heavy iron pot or deep skillet. Heat the oil and add the sliced celery. Cook, stirring frequently, for 10 minutes. Add the minced onion and cook for another 10 minutes. Remove the celery and onion from the pan. Add another tablespoon of olive oil. Heat the oil and add the cubed eggplant. Cook the eggplant over fairly high heat, stirring frequently, for 10 minutes. Return the celery and onion to the pan with the eggplant. Add the tomato sauce, salt, anchovy paste, capers, vinegar, water and basil to the pan. Simmer, uncovered, for 1/2 hour. Allow to cool to room temperature. Add the fructose. Store in the refrigerator. Serve cold as an appetizer before any Italian dish.

2 tablespoons olive oil
1 cup thinly sliced celery
1/2 cup minced onions
1 small eggplant, unpeeled and cut
   in 1-inch cubes (about 4 cups)
2/3 cup tomato sauce
1 teaspoon salt
1/2 teaspoon anchovy paste
2 tablespoons capers
3 tablespoons vinegar
1 cup water
1/2 teaspoon sweet basil
4 teaspoons fructose

Makes 12 servings
Each serving contains:
   1 Vegetable Exchange
   1/2 Fat Exchange
   48 calories

vegetables

artichokes, any number desired
2 garlic buds, peeled and halved
1 thick lemon slice
1/2 teaspoon salt
FRENCH or ITALIAN SALAD
    DRESSING, pages 62 and 63

1 artichoke contains:
    1 Vegetable Exchange
    25 calories

ARTICHOKE BOWLS
(for Soup or Salad)

Wash artichokes well and pull off tough outer leaves. Holding each artichoke by its stem, cut the tips off the leaves with scissors. When trimming the tops, start at the bottom of the artichoke and work your way to the top in a spiral pattern. Trim off the stem and turn artichoke upside down and press firmly to open it up as much as possible.

Pour water to a depth of 2 inches in the bottom of a saucepan. Add garlic, lemon slice and salt, then bring to a boil. Place artichokes in boiling water, cover tightly and cook over medium heat about 40 minutes or until stems can be easily pierced with a fork.

Remove artichokes from water and place upside down to drain until cool enough to handle easily. Remove the center leaves and spread the artichoke open very carefully. Reach down into the center and remove the furry choke, pulling it out a little at a time.

Place right side up in a glass baking dish. Pour a little FRENCH or ITALIAN SALAD DRESSING into each artichoke and allow to stand several hours in the refrigerator before serving.

My favorite first course is to serve soup and salad together. Place the marinated artichoke bowl on a plate. Fill with CONSOMMÉ MADRILÈNE, page 43, and top with 1 tablespoon of sour cream and 1/2 teaspoon caviar. On the side, heap a little sour cream dressing as a dip for the leaves. First, you eat your soup out of your artichoke bowl and then you eat the bowl for your salad.

Another unusual and delicious way to use the artichoke bowl is to fill it with seafood or chicken salad for a cold luncheon.

RICE AND VEGETABLES IN RED WINE

In a large, heavy iron skillet, melt the butter. Add rice, chopped tomatoes, sliced mushrooms and chopped onion. Cook for about 10 minutes, stirring occasionally. Add CHICKEN STOCK, wine, salt and pepper. Mix well. Cover and simmer for about 45 minutes or until rice is tender and all liquid is absorbed. Stir in peas and sprinkle Parmesan cheese on the top. Cover and heat thoroughly.

2 tablespoons butter
1 cup uncooked white rice
1 cup chopped tomatoes
4 cups (1 pound) sliced
    fresh mushrooms
1/2 cup finely chopped onion
3 cups CHICKEN STOCK, page 35
1/2 cup dry red wine
2 teaspoons salt
1/8 teaspoon freshly ground
    black pepper
1 cup cooked green peas
1/4 cup grated Parmesan cheese

Makes 6 servings
Each serving contains:
    1 Bread Exchange
    1 Fat Exchange
    2 Vegetable Exchanges
    165 calories

vegetables

4 tomatoes
1/2 cup buttermilk
1/4 cup grated Romano cheese
   (or Parmesan)
salt
freshly ground black pepper

1/2 tomato contains:
  1 Vegetable Exchange
  25 calories

16 large fresh mushrooms
2 buds garlic
2 sprigs fresh parsley
1/2 cup dry bread crumbs
1/2 cup grated Romano cheese
1/4 teaspoon oregano
1/4 teaspoon salt
1/8 teaspoon freshly ground pepper
4 teaspoons olive oil

Makes 8 servings
Each serving contains:
  1/2 Bread Exchange
  1/2 Fat Exchange
  1/4 Medium-fat Meat Exchange
  1/2 Vegetable Exchange
  89 calories

BUTTERMILK BAKED TOMATOES

Cut the tomatoes in half and remove seeds. (If very large tomatoes, cut in 1/2-inch slices.) Drip 1 tablespoon of buttermilk into each tomato half. Sprinkle the top of each with Romano cheese, salt and freshly ground pepper.

Put the tomatoes in a 400° oven for 15 minutes. Then put them under the broiler until lightly browned.

This is a delicious and colorful vegetable accompaniment for meats of all types.

Variations: Add a dash of oregano, basil, tarragon, garlic or rosemary if you wish. I like oregano with beef, rosemary with lamb and tarragon with chicken.

STUFFED MUSHROOMS

Wash mushrooms and remove stems. Put stems, garlic and parsley through a food grinder or chop cycle of a blender. Combine this mixture with the dry bread crumbs, Romano cheese, oregano, salt and pepper. Stuff this mixture into the mushroom caps. Drizzle the olive oil over each mushroom. Bake in a 350° oven for 40 minutes.

CAULIFLOWER INCOGNITO

Break cauliflower into flowerettes and cook in very little water until fork-tender. Mash it with a little of the water used for cooking. Add all the other ingredients and blend in a blender or whip with an electric beater until fluffy. Put the mixture in a casserole and bake at 350° for 20 minutes. Have fun while your guests wonder what this is!

Variations: Omit the nutmeg and onion. Add: 6 tablespoons grated Parmesan cheese and 1/4 cup minced green onion tops. Add 1/4 Medium-fat Meat Exchange and 18 calories.

1 large head cauliflower
1 tablespoon grated onion
1/4 teaspoon salt
1/8 teaspoon white pepper
1/8 teaspoon nutmeg

Makes 6 servings
Each serving contains:
    1/2 Vegetable Exchange
    12 calories

CREAMED SPINACH

Cook the chopped spinach and drain thoroughly. Add the BASIC WHITE SAUCE and Parmesan cheese and heat well together before serving.

Variation: Omit Parmesan cheese and add 1/8 teaspoon nutmeg. Each serving then contains 90 calories.

2 pounds fresh spinach, chopped
1-1/2 cups BASIC WHITE SAUCE,
    page 55
1/4 cup Parmesan cheese

Makes 6 servings
Each serving contains:
    1/2 Fat Exchange
    1/2 Whole Milk Exchange
    3/4 Vegetable Exchange
    128 calories

vegetables

1 cup uncooked white rice
2 tablespoons minced onion
2 cups CHICKEN STOCK, page 35
1 bay leaf

Makes 4 cups
Each 1/2 cup contains:
    1 Bread Exchange
    70 calories

1 cup uncooked white rice
2 tablespoons chopped onion
1 cup CHICKEN STOCK, page 35
1 cup tomato juice
1 bud garlic, minced
1/2 teaspoon salt
1/4 teaspoon oregano

Makes 4 cups
Each 1/2 cup contains:
    1 Bread Exchange
    70 calories

TOASTED PILAF

Spread the uncooked rice and onions in a pan with sides. Put the rice in a 400° oven, stirring frequently, until a golden brown. Cool. Place the rice and onion in a casserole with a cover and add the CHICKEN STOCK. Add the bay leaf. Cover and bake in a 350° oven for 30 minutes. Remove bay leaf before serving.

TOASTED MEXICAN RICE

Spread the uncooked rice in a baking pan. Put the rice in a 400° oven, stirring frequently, until a golden brown. Cool. Place the rice and onion in a casserole with a cover and add the CHICKEN STOCK, tomato juice, garlic, salt and oregano. Mix well. Cover and bake in a 350° oven for 30 minutes.

WILD RICE AND SESAME SEEDS

Wash the wild rice thoroughly in cold water. Drain well. Bring the CHICKEN BOUILLON to a boil. Add rice and cook over low heat, covered, until all the liquid is absorbed, about 40 minutes.

In a cured iron skillet, melt the butter. Add the toasted sesame seeds, onion and celery. Cook until the onion is clear and slightly browned. Add the cooked rice and mix well. Cook, uncovered, for 20 minutes, stirring frequently.

1 4-ounce package wild rice
1-1/2 cups CHICKEN BOUILLON, page 44
2 teaspoons butter
4 teaspoons TOASTED SESAME SEEDS, page 181
1/4 cup minced onion
1/4 cup minced celery

Makes 4 servings (2 cups)
Each serving contains:
   1 Bread Exchange
   1 Fat Exchange
   115 calories

MAMIE'S YAMS

Boil the yams with the skins left on until tender. Take them out of the water and cool. Peel the yams and mash them. Add orange juice, orange peel, vanilla, nutmeg, cinnamon and butter. Mix well. Beat the egg lightly. Mix the milk and fructose into the beaten egg and add this mixture to the yams. Beat with a rotary beater until fluffy. Bake at 325° for 20 minutes. Turn off the oven and leave the yams in it for 1/2 hour longer.

4 large yams
1 tablespoon orange juice
1 teaspoon grated orange peel
1 teaspoon vanilla
1/2 teaspoon nutmeg
1/4 teaspoon cinnamon
1 tablespoon butter
1 egg, lightly beaten
1/2 cup whole milk
2 tablespoons fructose

Makes 12 servings
Each serving contains:
   1 Bread Exchange
   1/4 Fat Exchange
   81 calories

sweets and desserts

Desserts are usually considered taboo in diabetic or reducing diets. However, the most refreshing and beautiful desserts imaginable are made with fruit, which is a necessary part of your diet program.

I have given you recipes for some fun, flamboyant and allowed desserts.

Surprise your friends with a towering GRAND MARNIER SOUFFLÉ or a FLAMING BAKED ALASKA, but day-in and day-out get in the habit of eating the wide variety of fresh fruits available to you all year.

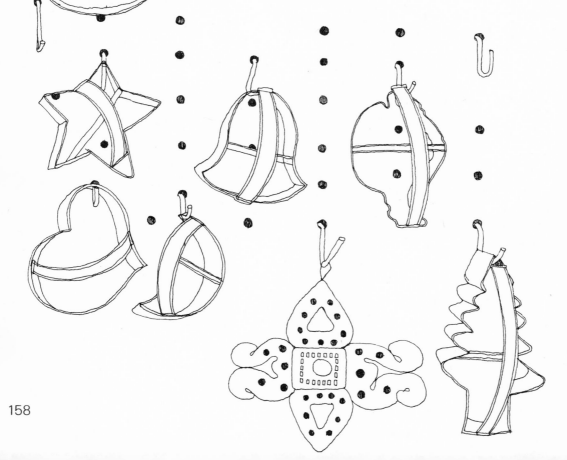

SOMETHING WITH NOTHING
(or a Smashing Spoof!)

Put the gelatin in a cup and soften with 1/4 cup cold water. Add boiling water and stir until the gelatin is completely dissolved. Add the sugar substitute and extracts. Put in the refrigerator until very firm.

When the mixture is firm, put into a blender. Add 1 cup cold water and blend on high speed until frothy. Pour into sherbet glasses and garnish with mint sprigs!

Variations: Instead of strawberry extract, any extract you wish may be substituted. For example:
• 1/2 teaspoon vanilla extract plus 1/2 teaspoon rum extract. Garnish with a dash of nutmeg.
• 1/4 teaspoon vanilla extract plus 1/2 teaspoon orange extract. Garnish with grated orange peel.
• 1/2 teaspoon vanilla extract plus 1 tablespoon grated lemon peel. Garnish with lemon twist.
• 2 teaspoons instant coffee plus 1/4 teaspoon cinnamon. Garnish with a small piece of cinnamon stick and a touch of WHIPPED MILK TOPPING, page 72.
• 1/4 teaspoon vanilla extract plus 1/2 teaspoon coconut extract. Garnish with crushed pineapple.
• 1/2 teaspoon vanilla extract plus 1/2 teaspoon almond extract. Garnish with WHIPPED MILK TOPPING, page 72, or pour a little milk over the top and sprinkle with a few raisins.

NOTE More than 1 serving must be accounted for as a partial Fruit Exchange.

1 envelope unflavored gelatin
1/4 cup cold water
3/4 cup boiling water
sugar substitute equal to
   1 tablespoon sugar
1/4 teaspoon vanilla extract
1 teaspoon strawberry extract
1 cup cold water

Makes 6 servings
One serving equals:
   FREE FOOD
   Calories negligible

159

6 small green cooking apples
2 cups water
2 teaspoons vanilla
1/2 teaspoon cinnamon
1/2 cup fructose

Makes 6 servings
1 small apple contains:
   2 Fruit Exchanges
   80 calories

BAKED CINNAMON APPLES

Wash and core the apples. Remove the peeling from the top 1/3 of each apple. Arrange the apples in a baking dish just large enough to hold them. In a saucepan bring the water, vanilla, cinnamon and fructose to a boil and pour over the apples. Put the apples in a 350° oven for 1 hour or until easily pierced with a fork. Baste the apples frequently while they are cooking. When apples are done, remove them from the oven and let cool in the sauce. They are good served either hot or cold. I love to serve Baked Cinnamon Apples warm with WHIPPED MILK TOPPING, sprinkled with cinnamon.

1 BAKED CINNAMON APPLE,
  preceding
1/4 cup cottage cheese
1/2 cup WHIPPED MILK TOPPING, 72
2 crushed graham crackers

Makes 1 serving
1 serving contains:
   2 Fruit Exchanges
   1 Low-fat Meat Exchange
   1/2 Whole Milk Exchange
   1 Bread Exchange
   290 calories

BREAKFAST BAKED APPLE
(Breakfast in a Dish)

Fill the center of the baked apple with cottage cheese. Pour the WHIPPED MILK TOPPING over the apple. Sprinkle the graham cracker crumbs on the top. You can alter this recipe to fit your diet for breakfast. For example, if you are allowed 2 Meat Exchanges instead of 1, you can have 1/2 cup cottage cheese instead of 1/4 cup. If you are allowed 2 Bread Exchanges, use 4 graham crackers instead of 2. If you need 1 Milk Exchange, pour 1 whole cup MILK TOPPING over the apple.

GRAND MARNIER SOUFFLÉ

Preheat the oven to 400°. Put 1 cup of milk on moderate heat so it will be at the boiling point when you need it. Melt the butter in a large saucepan, add the flour and stir for 3 or 4 minutes. Do not brown. Remove the butter-flour mixture from the heat and rapidly add all the boiling milk. Stir with a wire whisk until smooth. Return to the heat and bring to a boil, stirring constantly for 1 minute.

Remove from heat and add the egg yolks one at a time, stirring each one in thoroughly. Add 1/4 teaspoon salt, fructose, Grand Marnier and vanilla. I make this much of my dessert soufflé ahead of time. Then between the salad and the main course of the meal, put the egg whites in a large mixing bowl. Add the pinch of salt and cream of tartar. Beat the egg whites until they are stiff. Put 1/4 of the beaten egg whites in the re-warmed sauce and stir them in thoroughly. Add the remaining 3/4 egg whites and fold them in carefully. Do not over-mix! Pour the soufflé into an 8-inch soufflé dish and put it in the center of an oven preheated to 400°. Immediately turn the oven down to 375°. Cook for 20 minutes. Pour a little sauce over each serving. Serve immediately.

GRAND MARNIER SOUFFLÉ SAUCE

Mix together. Serve at room temperature, and don't tell anyone how you made it!

1 cup whole milk, boiling
4 teaspoons butter
2-1/2 tablespoons flour
4 egg yolks
1/4 teaspoon salt
1/4 cup fructose
2 tablespoons Grand Marnier or
   orange Curacao
1 tablespoon vanilla extract
5 egg whites
pinch salt
1/8 teaspoon cream of tartar

Makes 8 servings
Each serving including sauce contains:
   1/2 Fat Exchange
   1/2 Bread Exchange
   1/2 Medium-fat Meat Exchange
   1/2 Fruit Exchange
   116 calories

1 cup melted vanilla ice cream
1-1/2 teaspoons Grand Marnier

8 ripe, firm pears (Bartlett are best)
2 cups water
2 teaspoons vanilla extract
1 teaspoon rum extract
1/2 cup fructose
1/2 teaspoon cinnamon
4 drops red food coloring
nutmeg, for garnish

PARTY PEARS IN SAUTERNE SAUCE

Peel pears carefully, leaving the stems on them. With an apple corer remove the core from the end opposite the stem. Put the water, vanilla, rum extract, fructose, cinnamon and red food coloring in a saucepan and bring to a slow boil. Place the pears in the simmering water and cook, turning frequently, about 10 minutes or until easily pierced with a fork but not soft. Remove pears from heat and let cool to room temperature in the sauce. Cover and refrigerate all day or overnight in the sauce. Place each pear on a plate or in a shallow bowl and spoon a little SAUTERNE SAUCE over the top. Then sprinkle each serving with a touch of nutmeg.

1/2 cup sour cream
1/2 cup plain yogurt
2-1/2 tablespoons sauterne

Makes 8 servings
Each serving contains:
    2 Fruit Exchanges
    1/2 Fat Exchange
    102 calories

SAUTERNE SAUCE

Mix together and refrigerate all day or overnight before serving. Sauterne sauce is good on many other fruits.

CITRUS SAUCE COMPOTE

Grate the orange peel, being careful to use only the orange-colored part. Peel and dice the oranges over a bowl to catch the juice. Pour the juice in a saucepan. Add the grated orange peel, water, vanilla and ground cloves. Bring to a boil and boil for three minutes. Add the diced oranges and simmer for 10 more minutes. Cool and refrigerate. When cold, add fructose and mix well. Excellent served chilled as a light dessert. Try it in omelettes or as a sauce for French Toast and pancakes. Sometime, try it warmed on broiled chicken!

3 oranges
3 teaspoons finely grated orange peel
1/2 cup water
1/2 teaspoon vanilla extract
1/8 teaspoon ground cloves
2 teaspoons fructose

Makes 4 servings
Each serving contains:
    1 Fruit Exchange
    40 calories

BAKED RHUBARB

Wash and cut rhubarb. Grate orange peel, being careful to use only the colored part of the peel. Mix all ingredients together and put them in a casserole. Cover and bake at 350° for 40 minutes.

2 pounds rhubarb cut in 1-inch squares
    (4 cups)
2 teaspoons grated orange peel
2 tablespoons orange juice
3/4 cup fructose
4 drops red food coloring

Makes 8 servings
Each serving contains:
    1-1/2 Fruit Exchanges
    1/2 Vegetable Exchange
    73 calories

1 cup low-fat JELLED
    MILK, page 66
1-1/2 teaspoons fructose
1/2 teaspoon vanilla extract
1/2 cup cold low-fat milk
3 small ripe diced mangoes

Makes 6 servings
Each serving contains:
    1/4 Low-fat Milk Exchange
    1 Fruit Exchange
    71 calories

MANGO WHIP

Put all ingredients in the blender. Blend on high speed for 2 minutes, or until very frothy. Pour into 6 sherbet glasses and chill until set.

Instead of putting all the mango in the blender, you may want to put part of the diced mango in the bottom of each sherbet glass or bowl and pour the whipped mixture over it.

PINEAPPLE WHIP

Proceed as you do for MANGO WHIP (preceding page), except substitute for the mangoes 1-1/2 cups diced pineapple canned in natural juice and 1/2 teaspoon vanilla extract.

Makes 6 servings
Each serving contains:
    1/4 Low-fat Milk Exchange
    1/2 Fruit Exchange
    51 calories

FRESH PEACH WHIP

Proceed as you do for MANGO WHIP (preceding page), except substitute for the mangoes 3 diced medium-sized peaches, 1/4 teaspoon almond extract and 3/4 teaspoon fructose.

Makes 6 servings
Each serving contains:
    1/4 Low-fat Milk Exchange
    1/2 Fruit Exchange
    51 calories

FRESH STRAWBERRY WHIP

Put 1/4 cup sliced strawberries in the bottom of 6 sherbet glasses or bowls. Put the remaining 1-1/2 cups of strawberries in the blender with all of the other ingredients. Proceed exactly as you do for MANGO WHIP, page 164.

1 cup low-fat JELLED MILK, page 66
1/2 cup low-fat cold milk
3 cups fresh sliced strawberries
1-1/2 tablespoons fructose

Makes 6 servings
Each serving contains:
    1/4 Low-fat Milk Exchange
    3/4 Fruit Exchange
    61 calories

2 egg whites, lightly beaten
1 teaspoon vanilla extract
1/3 cup date "sugar"
1 cup peanut butter
2 tablespoons sifted flour

Makes 24 cookies
Each cookie contains:
   3/4 High-fat Meat Exchange
   1/4 Fruit Exchange
   79 calories

PEANUT BUTTER ICEBOX COOKIES

Combine egg whites, vanilla extract and date "sugar." Mix well and allow to stand for 10 minutes. Combine the egg white mixture, peanut butter and flour and mix thoroughly using a pastry blender. Form the dough into a ball and wrap tightly in wax paper or aluminum foil and refrigerate for at least 2 hours. Divide the cold dough into balls and place them evenly on 2 large cookie sheets. Press each cookie flat using the tines of a fork. Bake in a preheated 350° oven for approximately 12 minutes. Remove from the oven and allow to cool completely before removing the cookies from the cookie sheet. Be very careful handling the cookies as they are quite fragile and break easily.

SEMI-TROPICAL FRUIT CUP

Put yogurt and sliced banana in the blender. Blend until smooth. Pour banana-yogurt sauce over the diced orange and pineapple. Mix well and serve in sherbet glasses. Garnish with sprinkle of cinnamon and a mint leaf.

1/2 pint plain yogurt
1 ripe banana, sliced
1 orange, diced (a large navel orange
    is best)
1 cup diced pineapple (or unsweetened
    pineapple chunks cut in half)

Makes 6 servings
Each serving contains:
    1 Fruit Exchange
    40 calories

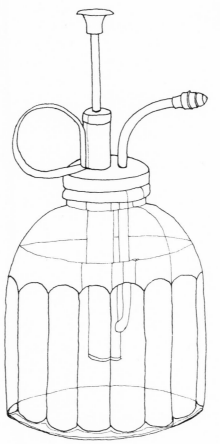

sweets/desserts

2 cups whole milk
1 teaspoon unflavored gelatin
1/4 cup fructose
1-1/2 teaspoons vanilla extract
dash salt

Makes 4 servings
Each serving contains:
   1/2 Whole Milk Exchange
   1 Fruit Exchange
   125 calories

CALCULATING ICE CREAM

Put 3/4 cup milk in the freezer until ice crystals form. Sprinkle gelatin over 1/4 cup milk in a cup. Scald the remaining 1 cup milk, then add the 1/4 cup milk with the gelatin to the hot milk and stir until the gelatin is dissolved. Allow to cool. When the milk is completely cool, add fructose, vanilla and salt. Pour into a freezer tray and freeze until firm, in a very cold freezer. Combine with the frozen 3/4 cup milk in a blender and blend until smooth and creamy. Pour back into the freezer tray and put in the freezer, turned low to freeze slowly. (If it doesn't freeze slowly, ice crystals will form.) After it is set, it may be stored in a normal freezer. Cover tightly with foil or wrap it in a plastic bag for storage. Remove from freezer 15 minutes before serving.

Variations: Fruit may be added to the ice cream before the first freezing. Half of the fruit may be added before the first freezing and the other half chopped and added after the ice cream is taken out of the blender. Or make original recipe and serve it topped with fresh fruit.

BAKED ALASKA

Prepare the ice cream and freeze. Beat the egg whites until they hold firm peaks. Remove ice cream from freezer, dip the bottom of the freezer tray in warm water and turn ice cream into an oven-proof serving dish.

Spread the egg whites on the ice cream like frosting. Put in under the broiler until lightly browned. You can put it back in the freezer until ready to use and run it under the broiler for 1 to 2 minutes just before serving. Divine with fresh fruit!

Variations: Just before serving, light 1/4 cup of brandy and pour over the top. Very dramatic!

1 recipe of CALCULATING ICE
 CREAM, page 168 (1 freezer tray)
3 egg whites

Makes 8 small servings
Each serving contains:
 1/4 Whole Milk Exchange
 1/2 Fruit Exchange
 62 calories

4 eggs
4 cups whole milk
1/4 teaspoon salt
1/4 cup fructose
1 teaspoon ground coriander
2 teaspoons vanilla extract
1 teaspoon rum extract
ground nutmeg

Makes 8 servings
Each serving contains:
    1/2 Medium-fat Meat Exchange
    1/2 Whole Milk Exchange
    1/2 Fruit Exchange
    142 calories

EGGNOG CUSTARD

Put all ingredients except nutmeg in the blender. Blend well. Pour mixture in a baking dish and sprinkle generously with ground nutmeg. Set the baking dish in a pan of warm water and bake in a preheated 250° oven for 2 hours, or until custard is firm. Cool to room temperature and then refrigerate until cold before serving.

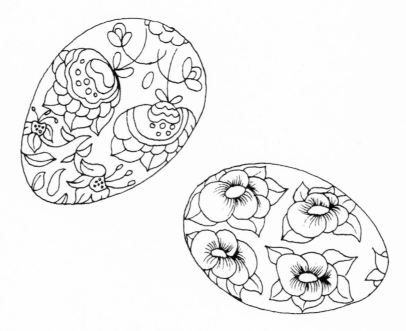

A cold, refreshing drink can range from a low-calorie drink to a meal in a glass. A nice hot drink can be calorie free or contain all of your allowed Fat Exchanges for the day. In this section, you will find a little bit of everything! Try them and then experiment with your own concoctions.

beverages hot and cold

beverages

1 cup low-fat milk
1/2 teaspoon vanilla extract
3/4 teaspoon fructose
3 or 4 ice cubes

Makes 1 serving
1 cup contains:
   1 Low-fat Milk Exchange
   1/4 Fruit Exchange
   135 calories

1 cup low-fat milk
3/4 teaspoon fructose
1/2 banana or 1 cup fresh strawberries
   or 1/2 cup pineapple or 1 fresh
   peach
1/4 teaspoon vanilla extract
3 or 4 ice cubes

Makes 1 serving
1 cup contains:
   1 Low-fat Milk Exchange
   1-1/4 Fruit Exchanges (depend-
     ing on how much fruit you use)
   175 calories

MILK FRAPPÉ

Put all ingredients in the blender and blend until the ice is pulverized and the drink is thick and foamy.

Variations: Use 1/4 teaspoon of any other extract you like, such as rum, mint, almond or strawberry.

Coffee Frappé Variation: Substitute 1 teaspoon instant coffee or Sanka for the vanilla extract. If you wish you may add 1/8 teaspoon cinnamon or 1/4 teaspoon rum extract.

FRUIT FRAPPÉ

Mix ingredients in the blender just as with the MILK FRAPPÉ. You can use a variety of fresh fruits. I just happen to like the ones listed above the best.

SALTY DOG

Squeeze the grapefruit juice. (Canned or frozen unsweetened grapefruit juice will do, but fresh grapefruit juice is best.) Rub the rims of 4 glasses with grapefruit juice and then dip each one in a plate of kosher salt. Add 1 ounce of vodka to each glass. Fill each with ice cubes and pour the grapefruit juice over the ice. This is a marvelous "before brunch" drink.

2 cups freshly squeezed grapefruit
   juice
Kosher salt
1 tray ice cubes
4 ounces vodka (optional)

Makes 4 servings
Each serving without vodka contains:
   1 Fruit Exchange
   40 calories
Each serving with vodka contains:
   140 calories

A COUNTERFEIT COCKTAIL

Pour the soda water over ice in a tall glass. Add the juice of 1/2 lime and a dash of bitters. Stir and serve.

This is also a good base for a gin or vodka cocktail.

1 tall glass soda water
1/2 fresh lime
Angostura bitters

FREE FOOD, calories negligible

173

beverages

1 teaspoon fresh lime juice
1/2 teaspoon Worcestershire sauce
1/4 teaspoon seasoned salt
dash freshly ground pepper
1 cup V-8 juice or tomato juice
dash Tabasco sauce (optional)
1 jigger (3 tablespoons) vodka
   (optional)

Makes 2 servings
tomato juice, 1/2 cup = 1 Vegetable
   Exchange, 25 calories
V-8 juice, 1/2 cup = 1 Vegetable
   Exchange, 25 calories
Each serving with vodka contains:
   125 calories

BLOODY MARY (With Vodka)
BLOODY SHAME (Without Vodka)

Mix the lime juice, Worcestershire sauce, seasoned salt and pepper together until the salt is dissolved. Add the V-8 or tomato juice and mix. Add the other two ingredients, if you are using them. Pour over ice and garnish with a celery stick for a stirrer.

RAMOS FIZZ (With Gin)
RAMOS FRAPPÉ (Without Gin)

Put fructose, milk, lemon and lime juice, orange flower water, egg white and 3 ice cubes in the blender. If you are using gin, add now. Blend until foamy. Pour over ice in 2 tall glasses. Add 2 tablespoons of soda water to each glass and stir a bit.

3/4 teaspoon fructose
1 cup whole milk
1 teaspoon lemon juice
1 teaspoon lime juice
4 drops orange flower water
1 egg white
1/4 cup soda water
1-1/2 ounces gin (optional)

Makes 2 servings
Each serving without gin contains:
   1/2 Whole Milk Exchange
   1/2 Medium-fat Meat Exchange
   122 calories
Each serving with gin contains:
   235 calories

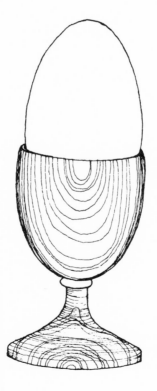

beverages

1 egg
1 cup whole milk
3/4 teaspoon fructose
1/2 teaspoon vanilla extract
1/4 teaspoon rum extract
1 ice cube
dash nutmeg

Makes 1 serving
Each Eggnog contains:
　1 Whole Milk Exchange
　1 Medium-fat Meat Exchange
　1/4 Fruit Exchange
　255 calories

EGGNOG

Dip the raw egg in boiling water for 30 seconds. Put the egg and all other ingredients in the blender and blend until the ice cube is pulverized and the Eggnog is frothy.

Pour into a glass and sprinkle with nutmeg.

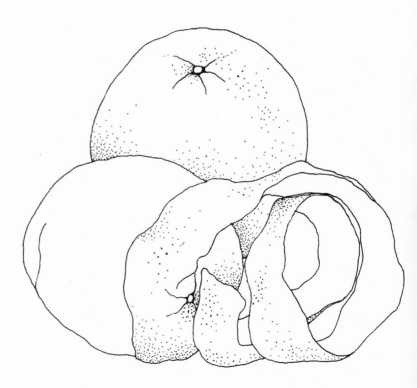

ORANGE CAESAR
(Breakfast in a Glass!)

Proceed exactly as for EGGNOG, preceding.

1 egg
1/2 cup whole milk
1/2 cup orange juice
3 tablespoons wheat germ, defatted
3/4 teaspoon fructose
1/4 teaspoon vanilla extract
1 ice cube

Makes 1 serving
Each Orange Caesar contains:
   1 Medium-fat Meat Exchange
   1/2 Whole Milk Exchange
   1-1/4 Fruit Exchanges
   1 Bread Exchange
   1 Fat Exchange
   325 calories

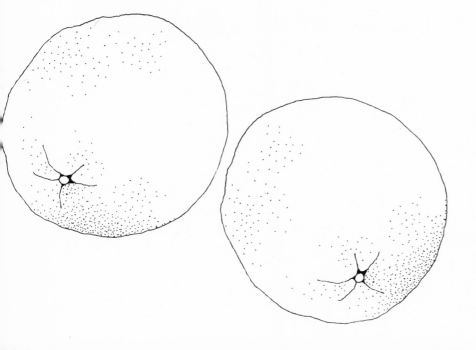

beverages

1/2 cup low-fat milk
1/2 cup orange juice
3/4 teaspoon fructose
1/4 teaspoon vanilla extract
3 ice cubes

Makes 1 serving
1 Orange Freeze contains:
    1/2 Low-fat Milk Exchange
    1-1/4 Fruit Exchanges
    112 calories

ORANGE FREEZE

Put all ingredients in the blender and blend until the ice cubes are pulverized and the drink is foamy.

Variations: Add 2 drops of orange flower water. Try substituting buttermilk for the milk. It's great!

1/3 cup pineapple juice
1/2 cup buttermilk
3/4 teaspoon fructose
3 ice cubes

Makes 1 serving
1 Pineapple Freeze contains:
    1/2 Non-fat Milk Exchange
    1-1/4 Fruit Exchanges
    90 calories

PINEAPPLE FREEZE

Proceed exactly as you do for ORANGE FREEZE.

DESERT TEA

Put the tea bags in 2-quart glass jars or bottles, fill with water and put the lids on the containers. Put the jars in the sun until the tea is the desired strength. This usually takes 2 hours, sometimes more, depending on strength of sun. Remove the tea bags and store the tea in the refrigerator. This is the best iced tea imaginable.

Variation: Add grated orange peel or crushed mint leaves to the water at the same time you put in the tea bags.

2 quarts cold water
2 tea bags

FREE FOOD, calories negligible

IRISH COFFEE

Pour the coffee into the glasses, add the fructose and Irish whiskey. Stir, and top with whipped cream. Remember whipping cream doubles in volume when whipped so 1/2 cup of cream will make 1 cup whipped cream; thus 2 tablespoons of whipped cream equal 1 Fat Exchange.

Variation: You may substitute 1/2 teaspoon rum extract for the Irish whiskey and call this Jamaican Coffee.

1 cup strong, freshly made coffee
  or Sanka
1-1/2 teaspoons fructose
1-1/2 ounces Irish whiskey
2 tablespoons whipping cream,
  whipped

Makes 1 serving
Each serving contains:
    1 Fat Exchange
    1/2 Fruit Exchange
    65 calories
Each serving made with Irish whiskey
contains:
    155 calories

calculating hints

CURING YOUR IRON SKILLETS

The purpose of "curing" your iron skillets is to use them for browning meat, cooking pancakes, omelettes and crepes, etc., without added fat. I prefer a "cured" iron skillet to Teflon because it's better for browning, and I don't have to worry about scratching it!

Take your new iron skillet, or your grandmother's old one, and put several tablespoons of oil in it. Put it on moderate heat and when it starts to get hot, tilt it from side to side until the oil coats the entire inner surface of the skillet. Continue heating the skillet until it gets so hot it starts to smoke. Then turn the heat off and cool the skillet. When it's cool enough to handle, wipe all the oil out of it with paper towels. Repeat this process three or four times, and you have a "cured" pan.

Never wash a "cured" pan with water. When you are through with it each time, wipe it out with oil. If anything is stuck on the bottom, rub it off with salt. If it is so bad that you have to wash it with water or if you use it for cooking liquids, all is not lost. Do not throw the pan away because it looks rusty, just cure it again!

I recently read an article in the San Diego Union quoting Dr. James Briggs, University of California nutritionist and president of the California Nutrition Council. He states that the amount of dietary iron in foods cooked in iron cookware is significantly higher than those cooked in aluminum, glass or coated cookware. He said "There is something in the way women used to cook. They stirred a lot and actually scraped a little iron off the skillet into the food. That is the kind of iron the body can use."

I was so pleased to learn that the skillets I had been using for years were good for my health as well as my cooking!

EGGS

You may wonder why all recipes in this book using a raw egg, say to coddle or dip the egg in boiling water for 30 seconds before using it.

The reason for this is that the avedin, a component of raw egg whites, is believed to block the absorption of biotin, one of the water soluable vitamins. Avedin is extremely sensitive to heat and coddling the egg inactivates the avedin.

Raw egg whites may be stored in the freezer and thawed before using.

VEGETABLES

Keep raw vegetables washed and ready to eat at all times. Then if you are hungry you can satisfy the nibbling urge with a nutritious low-calorie snack.

Keep minced parsley and chives in the freezer, for use when you need to season or garnish a dish quickly.

Also keep grated fresh ginger in the freezer. It is so much better than powdered ginger and is not always available in the market when you want it.

TOASTED NUTS AND SEEDS

Toast shredded coconut, chopped nuts, sesame seeds and sunflower seeds all in the same manner. Spread them thinly in a flat baking dish or cookie sheet with sides. Lightly salt them, (all but the coconut). Put them under the broiler. Watch them constantly because they will burn easily. Stir them around to brown evenly. When they are a golden brown, remove them. Cool and store in jars with tightly-fitted lids.

calculating hints

FAT CONTROL

To lower the amount of saturated fat in your diet, apply the following rules to your diet program.

1. Use liquid vegetable oils and margarines that are high in poly-unsaturated fats in place of butter. Two of the best oils for this purpose are safflower oil and corn oil.

2. Do not use olive oil, coconut oil or chocolate. (Many non-dairy creamers and sour cream substitutes contain coconut oil.)

3. Use non-fat milk.

4. Avoid commercial ice cream. Make CALCULATING ICE CREAM, page 168 using non-fat milk.

5. Limit the amount of beef, lamb, pork and ham in your diet to 4 or 5 times a week and eat more fish, chicken, veal and the white meat of turkey in its place.

6. Buy lean cuts of meat and trim all visible fat from the meat before cooking it.

CHOLESTEROL CONTROL

To lower the amount of cholesterol in your diet, apply the following restrictions to your diet program:

1. Limit or avoid egg yolks.

2. Limit shellfish such as oysters, clams, scallops, lobster, shrimp, and crab.

3. Limit or avoid organ meats of all animals, such as liver, heart, kidney, sweetbread and brains.

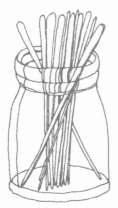

FRUCTOSE

In all recipes in this book which need to be sweetened I have used fructose rather than sucrose (ordinary sugar). Fructose is a natural fruit sugar which is far sweeter than sucrose. Because of this you use less of it and, therefore, automatically reduce calorie intake.

Fructose is absorbed more slowly from the intestinal tract than sucrose and therefore does not cause the equivalent sharp rise in blood sugar. Also, not all of it is metabolized as glucose in the liver.

One tablespoon of fructose must be counted as 1 Fruit Exchange in the diabetic diet. However, fructose is one-third sweeter than sucrose, so that if a recipe calls for 1 tablespoon of ordinary sugar (sucrose) you would use only 2 teaspoons of fructose.

DATE "SUGAR"

Date "sugar" is not really a sugar at all, although it looks and tastes very much like brown sugar. It is made by grinding dried dates to the consistency of coarse sugar and has the advantage of being allowed in sugar-restricted diets since it is just a ground fruit. One tablespoon of date "sugar" must be counted as 1 Fruit Exchange in the diabetic diet.

Date "sugar" is preferable to honey as a natural sweetener because honey is a refined carbohydrate. It is refined by bees for bees and it contains no fiber. Date "sugar" is not a refined carbohydrate, contains fiber and is lower in calories than honey.

Use date "sugar" just as you would use brown sugar on cereals and fruits. When baking with it, always add it to the liquid ingredient and allow it to stand for 10 minutes before combining the liquid with the dry ingredients. This will reconstitute the date "sugar" so that it does not cook faster than the other ingredients. When toasting date "sugar" with other ingredients, such as when making granola, add the date "sugar" about halfway through the total cooking time. This way it will not burn before the other ingredients are toasted.

183

table of equivalents

TABLE OF EQUIVALENTS

Avocado: 1 medium = 2 cups,
  chopped
Beets: 1 pound (medium) = 2 cups,
  cooked and sliced
Cabbage: 1 pound = 4 cups, shredded
Carrots: 1 pound (8 small) = 4 cups,
  chopped
Celery: 1 stalk = 1/2 cup, finely
  chopped
Corn: 6 ears = 1-1/2 cups, cut
Cucumber: 1 medium = 1-1/2 cups,
  sliced
Mushrooms, fresh: 1/2 pound (20
  medium) = 2 cups, raw, sliced
Mushrooms, dried: 3 ounces = 1 pound
  fresh
Onions: 1 medium = 1 cup, finely
  chopped
Peas, in pods: 1 pound = 1 cup, shelled
  and cooked
Potatoes: 1 pound (4 medium) =
  2-1/2 cups, cooked and diced
Spinach, fresh: 1 pound = 2 cups,
  cooked — 8 cups, fresh
Tomatoes: 1 pound (3 medium) =
  1-1/4 cups, cooked and chopped

DRIED VEGETABLES

Rice: 1 pound (2-1/2 cups) = 8 cups,
  cooked
Kidney beans: 1 pound (1-1/2 cups) =
  9 cups, cooked

Lima beans: 1 pound (2-1/2 cups) =
  6 cups, cooked
Navy beans: 1 pound (2-1/2 cups) =
  6 cups, cooked
Split peas: 1 pound (2 cups) =
  5 cups, cooked

FRESH FRUITS

Apples: 1 pound (4 small) =
  3 cups, chopped
Bananas: 1 pound (4 small) =
  2 cups, mashed
Berries: 1 pint = 2 cups
Cherries: 1 pint = 1 cup, pitted
Cranberries: 1 pound = 3 cups sauce
Grapefruit: 1 small = 1 cup, sectioned
Lemon: 1 medium = 3 tablespoons
  juice, 2 teaspoons grated peel
Orange: 1 small = 6 tablespoons juice,
  1 tablespoon grated peel
Papaya: 1 medium = 1-1/2 cups,
  chopped
Pineapple: 1 medium = 2-1/2 cups,
  chopped

DRIED FRUITS

Apricots: 24 apricot halves = 1 cup,
  uncooked = 1-1/2 cups, cooked
Dates: 1 pound (2-1/2 cups) =
  1-3/4 cups, pitted
Dates, pitted: 7-1/4-ounce package =
  1-1/4 cups, chopped

Figs: 1 pound (2-1/2 cups) =
  4-1/2 cups, cooked
Pears: 1 pound (3 cups) =
  5-1/2 cups, cooked
Prunes, pitted: 1 pound (2-1/2 cups) =
  3-3/4 cups, cooked
Raisins, seedless: 1 pound (2-3/4 cups)
  = 3-3/4 cups, cooked
Raisins, seedless: 15-ounce package =
  3 cups, not packed

MILK

Dry, whole powdered milk: 1/4 cup
  + cup water = 1 cup whole milk
Dry, non-fat powdered milk: 1/3 cup
  + 2/3 cup water = 1 cup non-fat
  milk

BREAD EXCHANGES

Crumbs

Bread crumbs, soft: 1 slice = 3/4 cup
Bread crumbs, dry, crumbled: 2 slices
  = 1/2 cup
Bread crumbs, dry, ground: 4 slices =
  1/2 cup
Graham crackers: 12 squares = 1 cup
  fine crumbs
Soda crackers: 21 squares = 1 cup
  fine crumbs

Cereals, Noodles

Arrowroot: 1-1/2 teaspoons =
  1 tablespoon flour
Flour, cake, sifted: 1 pound =
  4-1/2 cups

Bulgar: 1/3 cup = 1 cup, cooked
Cornmeal: 1 cup = 4 cups cooked
Cornstarch: 1-1/2 teaspoons =
1 tablespoon flour
Flour, all-purpose: 1 pound =
4 cups, sifted
Flour, cake, sifted: 1 pound =
4-1/2 cups
Macaroni: 1 pound (or 5 cups) =
12 cups, cooked
Noodles: 1 pound (or 5-1/2 cups) =
10 cups, cooked
Oatmeal, quick-cooking: 1 cup =
2 cups, cooked
Spaghetti: 1 pound = 9 cups, cooked

FAT EXCHANGES

Bacon: 1 pound, rendered =
1-1/2 cups fat
Butter: 1 cube = 1/2 cup or
8 tablespoons

NUTS IN THE SHELL

Almonds: 1 pound = 1 cup
nut meats
Brazil nuts: 1 pound = 1-1/2 cups
nut meats
Peanuts: 1 pound = 2 cups
nut meats
Pecans: 1 pound = 2-1/2 cups
nut meats
Walnuts: 1 pound = 2-1/2 cups
nut meats

NUTS, SHELLED

Almonds: 1/2 pound = 2 cups
Brazil nuts: 1/2 pound = 1-1/2 cups
Coconut: 1/2 pound = 2-1/2 cups,
shredded
Peanuts: 1/2 pound = 1 cup
Pecans: 1/2 pound = 2 cups
Walnuts: 1/2 pound = 2 cups

MEAT EXCHANGES

CHEESE AND CREAM

Cream cheese: 3-ounce package =
6 tablespoons
Cream, heavy whipping: 1 cup =
2 cups, whipped
Cottage cheese: 1/2 pound = 1 cup
Cheese, grated: 1/4 pound = 1 cup

EGGS

Eggs, raw whole: 6 medium = 1 cup
Eggs, raw in shell: 10 medium =
1 pound
Egg whites: 1 egg white, medium =
1-1/2 tablespoons
Egg whites: 9 egg whites, medium =
1 cup
Egg yolks: 1 egg yolk, medium =
1 tablespoon
Egg yolks: 16 egg yolks, medium =
1 cup

SEAFOOD AND FISH

Crab, fresh or frozen (cooked or
canned): 1/2 pound (5-1/2 - 7-1/2-
ounce tin) = 1 cup meat
Escargots: 6 snails = 1-1/2 ounces
Lobster, fresh or frozen (cooked):
1/2 pound = 1 cup meat
Oysters, raw: 1/2 pound = 1 cup
Scallops, fresh or frozen (shucked):
1/2 pound = 1 cup
Shrimp, cooked: 1 pound = 3 cups
Tuna, drained, canned: 6-1/2 - 7
ounces = 3/4 cup

MEAT AND POULTRY

Beef, cooked: 1 pound = 4 cups,
chopped
Beef, raw, ground: 1 pound = 2 cups
Beef, cooked, ground: 3/4 pound =
2 cups
Beef, raw, roast: 1 pound = 3/4 pound,
cooked*
1 whole chicken, canned (3 pounds,
4 ounces): 2 cups pieces without
skin or bones
Beef stock base, powdered: 1 teaspoon
= 1 bouillon cube
Beef stock base, powdered: 4 teaspoons + 1-1/4 cups water = 1 can
(10-1/2 ounces) beef bouillon,
undiluted

*Or 12 Exchanges

table of equivalents

Beef stock base, powdered: 1 teaspoon + 5 ounces water = 5 ounces
beef stock
Beef stock base, powdered: 1 teaspoon
+ 1 cup water = 1 cup beef bouillon
Chicken stock base, powdered: 1 teaspoon = 1 bouillon cube
Chicken stock base, powdered: 1 teaspoon + 5 ounces water = 5 ounces
chicken stock
Chicken stock base, powdered: 1 teaspoon + 1 cup water = 1 cup
chicken bouillon

FREE EXCHANGES AND SEASONINGS

BEVERAGES

Coffee: 1 pound (80 tablespoons) =
40-50 cups coffee
Tea leaves: 1 pound = 300 cups tea
Instant coffee: 4-ounce jar = 60 cups
coffee
Ice cubes: 2 ice cubes =1/4 cup
8 ice cubes = 1 cup

HERBS, SPICES, SEASONINGS

Garlic powder: 1/8 teaspoon =
1 small clove garlic
Ginger, powdered: 1/2 teaspoon =
1 teaspoon, fresh
Herbs, dried: 1/2 teaspoon =
1 tablespoon, fresh
Horseradish, fresh: 1 tablespoon =
2 tablespoons, bottled

MISCELLANEOUS

Baking powder: 1 teaspoon =
1 teaspoon baking soda plus
1/2 teaspoon cream of tartar
Chocolate: 1 square (1 ounce) =
4 tablespoons, grated
Chocolate: 1 square (1 ounce) =
3 tablespoons cocoa plus
1 tablespoons shortening

Gelatin sheet: 4 sheets = 1 envelope
Gelatin, powdered: 1/4-ounce envelope
= 1 scant tablespoon
Yeast, fresh: 1 package = 2 tablespoons
Yeast, dry: 1 envelope = 1-3/4 tablespoons to be reconstituted in
2 tablespoons water

CAN SIZES

6-1/2-ounce can = 3/4 cup (or
3 Meat Exchanges of tuna!)
8-ounce can = 1 cup
Number 1 can = 1-1/4 cups =
10-1/2 to 12 fluid ounces
12-ounce vacuum can - 1-1/2 cups =
12 ounces
Number 303 can = 2 cups =
16 to 17 ounces
Number 2 can = 2-1/2 cups =
20 ounces or 18 fluid ounces
Number 2-1/2 can = 3-1/2 cups =
27 to 29 ounces
Number 3 can = 5-3/4 cups =
51 ounces or 46 fluid ounces

index

index

index

biographical notes

JEANNE JONES has achieved an international reputation for combining creative cooking with sound nutritional practices. Following its publication in 1972, *The Calculating Cook* was approved for use by diabetics by the American Diabetes Association and named the best adult book of the year by the National Federation of Press Women. Subsequently she has published two other widely acclaimed books: *Diet for a Happy Heart* and *Fabulous Fiber Cookbook.*

Mrs. Jones' serious interest in nutrition started when she was placed on a diabetic diet herself and realized that this diet was not as restrictive as it first appeared, but rather just a perfectly balanced diet. Refusing to relinquish her role as a gourmet cook and hostess she used her international background in foods and entertaining to create a unique approach to recipes and menus for others on restricted diets.

Presently she serves as a consultant on recipe development and menu planning for a number of health organizations, diet-food manufacturers and restaurants. She is a member of the American Diabetes Association Committee on Foods and Nutrition, which revised the diabetic exchange lists in conjunction with the American Dietetic Association. She is also a member of the editorial board of *Diabetes Forecast* magazine and the External Advisory Committee to the Diet Modification Program of the National Heart and Blood Vessel Research Demonstration Center in Houston. Jeanne Jones is a frequent lecturer throughout the world in the field of diet and menu planning.

HOLLY ZAPP graduated in fine arts from the Syracuse University Art School. She has been an art director for several advertising agencies in San Francisco, where she now works as a free-lance artist and designer. She recently illustrated another 101 cookbook, *Jams and Jellies.*